Everything I Learned About Classroom Management,
I Learned in Puppy Class

A Guide to Positive Behavior Management in the Classroom

Dr. Shellie A. Harshberger

Copyright © 2026 by Dr. Shellie A. Harshberger

All rights reserved. No part of this book may be reproduced in any form or by any electronic or mechanical means, including information storage and retrieval systems, without permission in writing from the author, except by a reviewer who may quote brief passages in a review.

For permission requests, please contact the author.

ISBN: 979-8-9959174-0-3

Published by EDhanced Publishing

Printed in the United States of America

Table of Contents

Foreword

Okay, I lied. I did not learn *everything* I needed to know about classroom management in puppy class. What I did learn there, combined with educational psychology, years of classroom experience, and plenty of trial and error, taught me how to build positive relationships with students, keep order without losing my cool, and create the kind of environment where real learning happens.

Before I go further, let me pause to clarify. While this comparison might seem dehumanizing to some, I mean no disrespect. My pups are like my furry kids, and these stories serve only as a metaphor, a playful way to highlight truths about teaching. Students are not dogs, but both thrive when given patience, encouragement, and clear boundaries.

When I first drafted this idea nearly a decade ago, I had just adopted Sophie, a Doberman puppy with endless energy and zero patience for rules. At the same time, I was navigating the chaos of a new school year. As I worked with Sophie in puppy class, I was struck by how often the same principles applied to my classroom: consistency, clear expectations, patience, and, most importantly, reinforcing what I wanted to see instead of reacting to what I did not. Back then, this book began to write itself.

Then life happened. Sophie grew up, my career evolved, and the manuscript was shelved while I pursued more education. I earned my master's degree and my doctorate partly because I wanted to ensure that when I returned to this project, it would be more than funny and anecdotal. I wanted it to be relevant, research-based, and grounded in what truly works. I promised myself I would write this book someday.

Well, *someday* has arrived. Now, with nearly two decades of classroom experience, advanced study, and another dog in training, the parallels between teaching and dog training are as clear as ever. Dogs and students both crave structure and encouragement. They respond to positive reinforcement far better than punishment. They will test your patience, but persistence brings growth that makes the effort worthwhile.

Like every good training session, this book begins with structure, grows through trust, and ends with lasting leadership. Part 1, *Structure Breeds*

Security, explores how routines and consistency create safety and trust. Part 2, *Love 'Em to Learn 'Em,* turns to the heart of teaching, focusing on relationships, motivation, and connection. Finally, Part 3, *Leader of the Pack,* focuses on reflection, renewal, and the kind of leadership that sustains both teachers and students through the long walk together.

Across these chapters, you will find principles for effective classroom management paired with lessons from puppy class. You will see how consistency, subtle reinforcement, and patience build trust, how routines create structure, and how to redirect misbehavior without losing your sanity. Along the way, you will encounter real-life stories from my classroom and from my dogs, woven with insights from educational psychology and behavior management.

This book is part humor, part research, and all heart. At its core, teaching, like dog training, is about relationships built on trust, respect, and a few well-timed rewards to keep things interesting.

Part 1: Structure Breeds Security

Dog trainers often talk about the *Rule of 3* for rescues: it takes three days for a dog to start to settle, three weeks to feel comfortable, and three months to truly trust that this is home. The principle is simple but powerful. Time, consistency, and structure transform anxiety into security.

That same gradual shift from uncertainty to trust unfolds in our classrooms. Students arrive on the first day with nerves, curiosity, and their own version of puppy energy. They wonder, *What will this class be like? Will I succeed? Can I trust this teacher?* What happens in those first days and weeks lays the foundation for the rest of the year.

I think of this as the **First Day, First Week, First Month Rule**. On the first day, we establish initial routines. In the first week, we provide structure that fosters safety and belonging. By the first month, we begin to shape classroom climate, where routines and structure create consistency and predictability. Once those pieces are in place, it is time to solidify them, ensuring that consistency and predictability are built into every corner of classroom life.

This is the work of Part 1: Structure Breeds Security. It is where we provide the rules of the game. Just like a well-trained puppy learns where to go, what to do, and how to be part of the household, students learn what it means to be part of a classroom community. The chapters ahead will walk through that journey:

- **Puppergarten – Establishing Routines on the First Day**
- **Settling In – Structure Fosters Trust During the First Week**
- **Pack Rhythm – Building a Cohesive Community in the First Month**
- **Pavlov's Pup – The Psychology Behind Classroom Management**

Each step builds on the last. Boundaries and routines lay the foundation for freedom, safety, and trust. Once the rules of the game are understood, students can focus on what matters most: learning.

Chapter 1: Puppergarten – Establishing Routines on the First Day

The first day of school feels a lot like walking into puppy class, what I affectionately call *puppergarten*. Everyone is excited, a little nervous, and not entirely sure of the rules yet. Puppies bounce around, sniffing everything and everyone, eager to see what they can get away with. Students do the same thing, though in more subtle ways. Both are testing the boundaries of their new environment.

The lesson I learned in puppergarten is simple: what I allow on the first day is what I will live with all year. Just as a puppy who is permitted to jump on people in week one will keep jumping, a student who is allowed to disrupt or ignore routines on day one will keep doing it. Boundaries and expectations must be clear, consistent, and reinforced from the very beginning.

Why the First Day Matters

In puppy class, no one waits until week three to begin training. From day one, the puppy is learning what earns rewards and what leads to redirection. The same is true for students. The first day is a whirlwind of names, new schedules, and unfamiliar faces, and it is tempting to postpone rules and routines until things settle down. Yet students are already learning, from the very first moment, what kind of classroom this will be.

I once received an evaluation that said my class unfolded *"like a well-rehearsed play."* That assessment was not about my delivery of content but about the structure my students followed. They knew when to move, when to listen, and when to participate because those routines had been taught, practiced, and reinforced from day one. Students, like puppies, thrive on clarity. When they know what to expect, they can focus on learning instead of guessing at boundaries.

So how do we turn the first day into a foundation instead of a free-for-all? The answer lies in intentional, practiced routines that communicate stability and care.

Laying the Groundwork

The first day is not about content; it is about teaching students how to function in the classroom. This is where my **Tell, Model, Rehearse** approach shines. I begin by telling students my expectations for the start of class: check the whiteboard for supplies, take them out, and store backpacks at the front of the room. Then I model the process myself so there is no ambiguity. Finally, we rehearse it together, practicing the entrance procedure as we transition into assigned seats. This may sound tedious, but it is the single most important investment I make in those moments. Students are nervous, curious, and watching closely. They are learning not only the routines but also that I will be consistent, clear, and calm in guiding them.

Assigned seats are one of the most powerful classroom management strategies because they set the tone for order and intentionality. How we assign them matters. If we simply begin naming seats, chaos follows. Students jump up before we finish, chatter starts, and no one hears the rest of our directions. That is why I tell them: *"Now, before we rehearse the entrance procedure, I am going to give you your assigned seat. This will be a bit like Simon Says, because your job is to look and listen, but do not move until Simon, also known as Mrs. H, says."* This playful approach prevents confusion, builds listening skills, and makes clear from the first day that structure is a priority. It also communicates something deeper: every student has a place in this room. No one is left to wander or wonder where they belong. Over time, the seating chart also allows me to be intentional about partnerships, proximity, and classroom dynamics. When I need to adjust seats later in the year to address side chatter or encourage collaboration, students are already accustomed to the idea that where they sit matters and that those decisions are made with purpose. Skipping this step on the first day leaves too much to chance, and chance rarely builds the kind of environment students need to thrive.

Once students are comfortable in their designated seats, I introduce dry-erase name plates. Each student writes their preferred name in large, clear letters and adds a quick emoji to show how they feel that day. While they work on a short prompt, I use this time to circulate the room and offer individualized one-on-one greetings. These brief check-ins let me connect with students personally and set a tone of respect and attentiveness. The routine continues long after I know everyone's names because its value reaches far beyond identification. From the very start, students see that I care about who they are and how they feel. The name plates, combined with the daily greetings, communicate two powerful messages: your name matters, and your feelings matter.

Over time, the emojis give me daily snapshots of the class's emotional climate. A row of tired faces after a late-night game or a string of sad faces after a difficult community event tells me I may need to adjust my approach that day. Sometimes I quietly check in with a student whose emoji signals more than they are ready to say out loud. What begins as a lighthearted routine on the first day grows into a meaningful practice of relationship-building and emotional awareness that strengthens the classroom culture.

The first day is also when I establish the cell phone policy. I never wait until it becomes an issue because by then I am reacting instead of leading. Once students are settled into their seats and name plates are complete, I explain exactly how phones will be managed. Each student has a "parking spot" for their phone on their desk. If a phone is out during class, I quietly place a pencil bag on that student's desk. Without words, this signals that the phone needs to go inside the bag until the end of class. This policy is simple, non-confrontational, and effective.

Then, just like any other procedure, we practice it together using the **Tell, Model, Rehearse** approach. I explain the expectation, demonstrate it myself, and then we all rehearse it until it feels natural. This consistency prevents me from becoming the "phone police" later in the year. Students know the system, they know it will be enforced the same way every day, and most don't test it. Clear procedures for phones also communicate respect: I am not banning technology outright, but I am setting boundaries so we can focus when we need to. By practicing this routine on the very first day, I send the message that learning time is valuable and protected.

Alongside routines for seats, name plates, and phones, I also teach what I call my **Listening Rule**. I tell students, *"In my classroom, when I am talking, you are listening and showing me with your eyes that I have your attention."* This communicates that listening is not passive, it is active. It is demonstrated by quiet mouths and attentive eyes. I also make it clear that this expectation goes both ways. I will not talk over students, and when they speak, they will have my full attention. From the very beginning, this sets a tone of mutual respect and reinforces that everyone's voice matters.

By the end of the first day, students have experienced more than rules. They have practiced the rhythms that will guide our entire year together. From entering the room to finding their seats, from sharing their names and feelings to managing phones and listening respectfully, each step communicates that this classroom is structured, safe, and intentional. None of it is left to chance.

The challenge, of course, is that students quickly learn not only from what we teach intentionally, but also from what we reinforce in the moment. Real-time reinforcement has the power to shape behavior immediately, and the first day offers countless opportunities to strengthen the habits we want or unintentionally cement the ones we do not.

Reinforcement in Real Time

Dog trainers know that feedback must be immediate. Correct or reward too late, and the puppy no longer connects the action to the consequence.

In the classroom, reinforcement works the same way. We can only reinforce behavior that is happening in the moment. If a student is focused while others are distracted, we can walk by quietly, drop a sticker on the desk, and whisper, *"Thanks for working hard."* They feel seen, and the others notice without embarrassment. This kind of subtle, immediate reinforcement is powerful. Most students want recognition, but not the spotlight. A quiet nod or a smile can carry more weight than a loud *"Great job!"* shouted across the room.

The principle is universal: reinforcement works best when it is quick, quiet, and specific. Of course, reinforcement cuts both ways. When we are not intentional, we can just as easily reinforce the very behaviors we do not want. I learned this lesson the hard way with a student we will call Adam.

Adam and the Jackpot of Attention

In dog training, one mistake owners often make is accidentally rewarding behavior they don't want. Petting the puppy who jumps, for example, ensures that the jumping continues.

I made this mistake myself with Adam. On the first day of class, Adam began making witty comments out-of-turn. They were not malicious, and I, trying to build rapport, smiled and occasionally responded. Without realizing it, I was reinforcing his interruptions. Each smile was a jackpot. By the next class, his behavior was already cemented.

This is a classic example of operant conditioning: behavior followed by reinforcement increases in frequency. What I had intended as friendliness became fuel for disruption. Adam was gambling for attention, and because I sometimes paid out, he kept trying.

Puppies and students both repeat what is rewarded. But here is the critical difference: puppies grow out of puppyhood. Students grow into adulthood, carrying the lessons we taught, intentionally or unintentionally, about what earns attention. If we want a classroom that is focused and respectful, our reinforcement must match the behaviors we want to see repeated.

Research Spotlight: Reinforcement Works

B. F. Skinner (1953) demonstrated through his operant conditioning experiments that behavior reinforced immediately and consistently is more likely to be repeated. Furthermore, Marzano et al. (2003) found that consistent classroom routines and reinforcement can increase instructional time by up to 25 percent, simply by reducing disruptions. Together, these findings confirm what teachers experience daily: attention is powerful currency, and how we spend it determines the climate of our classroom.

Research shows us what works, but how we deliver it matters just as much. Reinforcement and routines are only effective when paired with the calm, steady presence of the teacher.

The Teacher as a Calm Guide

A good trainer in puppergarten is calm, patient, and consistent. Puppies take their cues from the energy of the person guiding them. In the same way, a classroom mirrors the tone of its teacher. Our calm becomes their calm.

Authority in the classroom does not come from volume or intimidation. It grows from consistency paired with steady, collected care. Students are highly attuned to emotional shifts. When guidance is calm and predictable, they feel secure. When frustration takes over, focus erodes and behavior follows suit. What students respond to most is not intensity, but steadiness.

Calm, intentional guidance earns respect and builds trust. Just as puppies look for reassurance in a trainer's tone and posture, students find security in a teacher who remains grounded under pressure. In that steadiness, authority is reinforced, learning feels safe, and composure teaches far more than words ever could.

Practical Puppergarten Strategies

The first day of school is the classroom's own version of puppergarten. This is the moment to introduce the boundaries, routines, and expectations that will become the foundation for the year. Just as a puppy learns where to sit, when to wait, and how to respond to cues, students begin learning how the classroom operates from the moment they walk in.

Here are four principles to guide the first day:

1. **Teach Procedures Like Lessons**
   Avoid assuming students know how to enter, gather supplies, or listen attentively. Use the **Tell, Model, Rehearse** approach: teach the behavior explicitly, model it, and then rehearse it with students until it feels smooth and predictable.

2. **Model the Desired Behavior**
   Demonstrate respect, patience, and focus. Students watch closely, more than we realize. Therefore, what we model in tone, posture, and clarity becomes the standard they follow.

3. **Reinforce Immediately**
   Acknowledge correct behavior the moment it appears. Preparation, cooperation, and attentiveness deserve quick recognition so students understand what earns attention.

4. **Direct Attention Purposefully**
   On the first day, attention is the strongest reinforcer we have. Smiling at witty interruptions or responding to off task behavior can accidentally encourage it. Instead, focus attention on students who are meeting expectations so the class learns what truly matters.

Closing Reflection

Puppergarten taught me that setting boundaries is about creating a safe space for growth. Puppies given structure can explore confidently without chaos. Similarly, students given routines and expectations can take academic risks without fear.

The first day of school is our puppergarten. It sets the tone for everything that follows. We teach expectations as intentionally as we teach content. We **Tell, Model, and Rehearse**. We reinforce what we want to see. We stay calm, stay consistent, and remember: what we allow now is what we will live with all year.

The habits we build together on the first day become the heartbeat of the year ahead.

Reflection Questions

1. What are three specific routines you want your students to master on the first day of school?
2. Can you think of a time when you accidentally reinforced a behavior you did not want? How could you prevent it in the future?
3. In your classroom, how do you currently acknowledge students who are meeting expectations? In what ways does your reinforcement reflect immediacy, subtlety, and specificity, and where might it fall short?
4. If someone observed your class on the first day, what impression would they form of your routines and expectations?
5. How could you strengthen your own puppergarten to set a stronger tone for the year?

Try This Tomorrow

Entrance Routine Drill

- Write the day's needed supplies on the board.
- As students enter, have them practice gathering materials, storing book bags, and preparing for class.
- Reinforce the students who complete the routine with a quiet *"thank you"* or subtle recognition.

Chapter 2: Settling In – Structure Fosters Trust During the First Week

Bringing home a new puppy is exciting and rewarding, but it is also messy. Anyone who has navigated puppy training and housebreaking knows the truth. If we do not establish structure immediately, we will spend weeks cleaning up after accidents. Puppies thrive on predictable routines. They go out at the same times each day, they are praised in the right moments, and they are gently redirected when they miss. It is not glamorous work, but it builds security and trust.

The same is true in the classroom. Students crave a safe and structured environment where expectations are clear. Without it, small disruptions turn into major messes, and learning quickly gets lost in the chaos. Our job, much like the new puppy owner guiding their dog into good habits, is to create an environment where accidents are minimized, success is reinforced, and routines become second nature.

Securing Attention

The first week is when we begin to shape not just routines, but the attention habits that make those routines possible. Even the most consistent structure will fail if students are not tuned in to us when it matters. Puppies learn quickly that a command only works when their eyes and ears are on the trainer. Similarly, the same principle applies to our students. Before we can expect predictability or consistency, we must first secure their attention.

What began on the first day continues into the first week as I solidify the **Listening Rule**: when I am speaking, students are not. Their eyes are on me, and their bodies show signs of active listening. I do not talk over side chatter or begin instructions while Chromebooks are open or phones are in use. Instead, I pause, wait calmly, and signal that attention is required before we move forward. This quiet patience sends a clear message: listening comes first.

Just as important, I remind myself that when I ask for their attention, I must have something worth their focus. If I demand attention only to fumble with materials or repeat unclear directions, I weaken the expectation

I have set. Organization and preparation on my part show students that paying attention pays off.

By building these habits during the first week, students learn that focus is not optional. It is the foundation. Once attention is secured, routines gain traction, consistency becomes visible, and predictability begins to feel safe. Without this step, everything else risks being noise.

Reinforcing Trust in the First Week

By the end of the first week, I expect most routines to be consistent. For instance, students should know how to enter the classroom, gather supplies, park their phones, and sit in their assigned seats with name plates ready.

The first week is also when I introduce the **Thank You Slip**. This is a small preprinted note, usually on bright or colorful paper, that functions much like a treat in puppy class. It quietly says, *"I see you, and I am happy with your behavior."* Early on, the slip has no additional reward. Later, it may be connected to privileges, but in the first week it is purely symbolic. Its power lies in the message it sends.

These early routines show students that expected behavior earns attention and recognition. Behavior that does not align is ignored. The student simply misses out on the quiet acknowledgment others receive. This is the heart of the first week. We are teaching students exactly which behaviors will earn attention and which behaviors will not. Just as puppies repeat actions that earn them treats, students repeat actions that earn them meaningful recognition.

Thank You Slips also build mutual respect. Students know their efforts will be noticed, and we show that recognition is steady and fair. This gentle pattern of reinforcement sets the stage for the predictability students need to thrive.

The Power of Predictability

In dog training, the first step is consistency. Out every two hours, same door, same command. The predictability helps the puppy understand what is expected. Without that consistency, the puppy is left to guess, and guessing rarely ends well.

Likewise, inconsistency affects students just as strongly. When the school day feels unpredictable, such as when expectations shift without clarity, or when students are permitted to talk out of turn at times and corrected at others, students feel unsettled. Some will test the limits; others will withdraw. Importantly, what all of them need is the comfort of knowing exactly how things work in the classroom every day.

The first week is when we build trust through consistent structure and by reinforcing, again and again, every routine we introduced on the first day. Through this process, students learn that structure creates stability and allows them to focus on learning rather than guessing what comes next. In addition, they learn that expectations are not temporary rules, but the foundation of how the class operates. When students see that we mean what we say, confidence grows and behavior aligns.

Consistency is the Key

The opposite of predictability is inconsistency, and inconsistency teaches the wrong lesson. I once knew a family whose children were out of control. Their antics could be outrageous. Once, they even crunched up a bag of chips and poured it into their grandparents' bed. Their mother responded in unpredictable ways. Sometimes she laughed at their behavior. Other times she punished them harshly. The children did not learn how to behave. Instead, they learned how to avoid making their mother angry.

Inconsistency sends the same message in the classroom, and students respond accordingly. When expectations are reinforced one day but ignored the next, students stop focusing on the behavior and start focusing on the teacher's mood. The result is confusion, wasted time, and a loss of trust. Conversely, when procedures and rules are enforced consistently and calmly, students know exactly what to expect. They begin to trust that good behavior will always be recognized and poor behavior will always be corrected in the same way.

Consistency is about reliability. When students trust that the rules are steady and predictable, they are free to focus on learning instead of trying to figure out what kind of day it is going to be. Consistency also requires us to project confidence and never lose our cool. Students watch us carefully, and they take their cues from how we respond. If we wobble, they wobble. If we stay calm and firm, they feel secure.

Procedures are the Foundation

Puppies learn through step-by-step housebreaking routines. We do not just hope the puppy figures it out. We teach. We guide. We repeat.

In the classroom, procedures function the same way. Students cannot be expected to instinctively know how to transition, collaborate, or participate respectfully. We must teach these skills as intentionally as we teach math problems or lab techniques.

This is where I take time to explain my "why." Students need to know that routines and structures are not arbitrary. They are designed to create safety, fairness, and space for everyone to learn. When we explain *why* our procedures exist, students see them as part of the learning culture rather than hoops to jump through.

This is also the time to continue building on relationship routines such as one-on-one check-ins with emoji name plates. Even though I know their names by now, the practice communicates that emotions matter. These quick personal check-ins, paired with consistent routines, build trust that I see students as individuals, not just as members of a group.

The Timer – A Nonverbal Manager

Once students are familiar with my **Tell, Model, Rehearse** strategy, usually within the first week, I introduce a timer. The timer ensures that procedures are completed within clear time frames. It provides structure and consistency, turning routines into predictable patterns the whole class can trust. Here are a few moments where the timer makes the biggest impact:

- **Entering the Classroom**: Once the bell signals the start of class and students are secure with the entrance procedure, I project a two-minute timer as they enter. Their task is to read the whiteboard, gather materials, and place their backpacks at the front before the timer expires. When the timer hits zero, students know to be seated and ready. As a result, the clock becomes a clear cue for order and readiness to learn.

- **Transitions**: Once basic routines are comfortable, I layer in timers to keep movement purposeful. If students are shifting to lab groups, they get ninety seconds. If they are pair-sharing, they have two minutes. When the timer beeps, everyone immediately returns to their seat with eyes on me. This prevents the slow drift of "just one more minute" and keeps transitions efficient and focused.

- **End of Class**: Dismissal is also a procedure. Students work until the timer signals that cleanup should begin. They have a set amount of time to return supplies and sit again. Bags stay at the front of the room until I direct otherwise. Sometimes I release students by table groups, levels of participation, or correct answers to review questions. Regardless of the method, students know that release always comes from me, and the timer cues each phase.

Through these procedures, the timer becomes a nonverbal classroom manager. It signals how long students have, when to stop, when to return attention to me, and when to move on. It also allows for pause, look, and listen moments, allowing me to reveal new information with intentional timing. With that comes the caveat. If I expect students to pause and listen, I must be prepared. What I share in these moments must always be worthy of their attention.

The Order of Instructions Matters

One of the most overlooked aspects of classroom management is the sequence of events. A common mistake is passing out materials before giving directions. The moment students have a paper in their hands, their eyes drop. It is human nature to look at what you have been given, and attention is immediately split.

This is not just a student issue. It happens to adults too. I have sat through professional development sessions where the presenter handed out a packet before explaining the activity. Within seconds, the room was filled with the sound of papers flipping, whispered questions about the task, and people skipping ahead. No matter how engaging the speaker was, they had lost the room. The mistake was not about the activity; it was about poor timing.

In the classroom, this mistake costs instructional time and undermines authority. When we want students to listen, we must instruct first, then give the tangible item. It seems simple, but it is a discipline of sequencing. By holding back the material until after directions are clear, we preserve attention, reduce confusion, and set the expectation that listening comes before doing.

Just as a puppy learns to sit before receiving a treat, students learn that attention comes first. Over time, this sequence builds smoother lessons, stronger focus, and deeper respect for the flow of instruction.

Research Spotlight: Sequencing and Routines

Barak Rosenshine's (2012) *Principles of Instruction* emphasize sequencing and modeling as essential tools for reducing confusion and strengthening comprehension. Furthermore, research confirms that when teachers give instructions before distributing materials, students' attention remains focused rather than split. Cognitive research supports this: our working memory is easily overloaded when multitasked, so even the small distraction of receiving a paper at the wrong time reduces listening and retention (Sweller et al., 2019).

As previously noted, Marzano et al. (2003) demonstrated that teachers who establish and maintain clear routines can increase instructional time by as much as 25 percent. Without predictable routines, valuable minutes are lost each day to confusion, transition noise, or redirection. Over a school year, this adds up to weeks of lost instruction. Therefore, establishing structure early is not just about behavior, it is about reclaiming time for learning.

Together, sequencing and routines show that small details matter. The order in which instructions are given, the consistency of procedures, and the way time is managed are not trivial. They are powerful tools for preserving instructional flow and maximizing the time students spend engaged in meaningful learning.

Practical Settling-In Strategies

Just as puppies learn best with structure and repetition, students thrive in classrooms where routines are predictable and safety is prioritized. The timer is an ally in this process.

1. **Establish Nonnegotiables**
   Identify the routines that matter most for safety and order, such as entrance procedures and securing attention. Reinforce them daily until they become automatic.

2. **Use a Timer as a Nonverbal Manager**
   Use the timer as both a pacing tool and a signal for order. Teach students that when the timer reaches zero, there is a clear next step, such as pausing, returning to their seats, or directing attention to you.

3. **Rehearse with Consistency**
   The first week is about practice, not perfection. Rehearse each routine, whether entrance, transition, or dismissal, until it becomes smooth. Additionally, pair every rehearsal with clear cues and meaningful reinforcement.

4. **Reinforce Immediately and Often**
   Notice when students follow routines within the time given. A nod, a quiet "*thank you*," or even a first release for bag retrieval signals success. In the first week especially, reinforcement must be frequent so students clearly see the link between action and recognition.

5. **Correct Calmly**
   Treat mistakes as part of the process. Reset the timer, try again, and reinforce success when it occurs.

Closing Reflection

The first week is about proving to students that they can trust the classroom environment. Trust grows when our words match our actions, when routines are reinforced consistently, and when expectations remain clear every single day. Just as puppies relax when they know when to eat, play, and rest, students thrive when they know how class begins, how transitions happen, and how lessons wrap up.

The timer is one way we make this structure visible. It signals when to start, when to pause, and when to wrap up. Beyond that, it reassures students that the classroom follows patterns they can count on. Whether through a timer, clear instructions, or practiced routines, the message is the same. You can feel safe here because you know what to expect.

Ultimately, structure gives students a sense of stability. When they trust the flow of the day, they stop testing boundaries and start focusing on learning. During the first week, consistent routines show that the classroom operates in clear and reliable ways. In turn, students learn they can count on the process we have established, and that predictability gives them the confidence to invest their energy in learning rather than uncertainty.

Reflection Questions

1. What routines do you establish during the first week that signal to students they can trust the structure of your classroom?
2. How do you explain the "why" behind your routines so students understand their purpose rather than viewing them as arbitrary rules?
3. In what ways do you signal attention, such as a timer, verbal cue, or nonverbal gesture, and how consistent are you with these signals?
4. Think of a time when inconsistency in your classroom created confusion. How might predictability have changed that outcome?
5. How do your procedures free students to focus on learning rather than on figuring out what is expected?

Try This Tomorrow

Trust Through Structured Practice

- Choose one routine students will use every day, such as entrance, transitions, or dismissal.
- Explain why the routine matters for learning and safety so students understand its purpose.
- Use the **Tell, Model, Rehearse** approach to walk them through it step by step.
- Layer in a consistent signal, such as a timer, raised hand, or call-and-response, to mark the start and end of the procedure.
- Quietly reinforce students who follow the routine exactly as practiced.

Chapter 3: Pack Rhythm – Building a Cohesive Community in the First Month

Bringing a puppy into a household is one thing, but helping that puppy settle into the rhythm of the "pack" is another. The first month is when the novelty wears off, boundaries are tested, and habits begin to harden. A well-socialized puppy learns how to belong, not just with its owner but within the pack.

The first month in a classroom mirrors this same shift from novelty to belonging. This is where order is established and community takes root. Students begin testing limits, gauging whether our rules still matter, and watching closely to see if we follow through. This is where structure deepens into culture. Our goal in this stage is to ensure that teacher–student, student–student, and teacher–parent relationships are aligned in a way that builds trust, respect, and cohesion.

Teacher-Student Relationships: Following Through with Care

By the first month, students are comfortable enough to test boundaries. This is the moment where many teachers give in, but the message is clear: if we do not uphold the expectations we set, students lose respect.

We must continue to boldly wait for conversations to stop, for eyes to turn toward us, and for body language to show active listening. Sometimes this requires patience; other times it requires creativity. A playful, *"Oh, how I wish EVERYONE was looking at me so I could begin our lesson,"* may work one day. On another, walking slowly toward the off-task student communicates seriousness without raising our voice. Proximity is powerful.

For persistent issues, even the timer can become an ally. Allowing an obnoxious beep to continue until every student follows directions, while calmly narrating, *"I so wish I could turn off this timer, if only everyone was ready,"* often prompts peer accountability. This relentlessness, done with patience and good humor, sends a consistent message: our expectations are not negotiable, and they will be upheld.

One-on-one greetings also remain powerful during this stage. While they do not have to happen daily, they can occur more frequently at first and then taper to once a week. These moments reinforce individual value and continue to humanize the classroom, reminding students that they are seen as people, not just learners.

While holding the line with care strengthens the teacher–student relationship, community does not stop there. A truly cohesive classroom is not built solely on the relationship between the teacher and students, but on the ways that students treat and learn from one another. Just as a pack of dogs learns to move in sync, our students need structures that help them collaborate respectfully, share responsibility, and trust each other. This is where intentional peer-to-peer strategies become essential.

Student-Student Relationships: Structuring Collaboration

Within the first month, it is essential to foster student-student relationships. Even with strong teacher–student trust in place, a classroom will not thrive unless students learn how to collaborate productively. Left unchecked, group work can easily slide into one student doing all the work, or worse, groups functioning as cliques that exclude others. That is why I establish collaboration norms and structured practices right away. These set the tone for how students will work productively and how they will treat one another all year long.

Collaborative Norms: Setting the Ground Rules

Before diving into specific collaboration strategies, it is essential to establish what productive collaboration actually looks like. Students often think working together means sharing answers or letting the strongest student carry the group. That is not collaboration; that is avoidance. On the other hand, when we set clear ground rules, students learn that collaboration is about **shared thinking, not shared copying**.

In my classroom, acceptable collaboration means explaining reasoning out loud so peers can follow the thought process, pointing out where answers are found in the text or notes, paraphrasing together, and asking clarifying questions such as *"Can you show me how you set that up?"* or *"Why did you do it that way?"* It also means dividing roles fairly in projects, using sentence starters like *"I think another way is…"* or *"I disagree because…"* to keep dialogue respectful, and checking in with one another's progress.

Unacceptable collaboration, on the other hand, includes passing a paper over for someone else to copy, letting one group member do all the work, or refusing to contribute. It also includes dismissing another student's idea without explanation, ignoring assigned group roles, or going off-task so that others are left to carry the load.

By taking time to define these norms, we set a foundation that prevents misunderstandings later. Furthermore, students come to see collaboration not as an easy shortcut, but as a structured process that demands accountability, respect, and shared effort. Once these expectations are clear, collaborative lessons have a greater chance of succeeding because everyone understands the difference between meaningful collaboration and simple convenience.

With these norms in place, students need repeated opportunities to practice working with different classmates. One of the simplest and most effective is clock partnering.

Clock Partnering: Building Flexibility and Connection

Rather than allowing students to drift toward the same familiar faces, clock partnering gives structure to pairing while still keeping it lighthearted and fun. Traditionally, the activity involves creating a clock with twelve appointment slots, but in my classroom, I simplify it by designating just a few key times such as 12:00, 6:00, and 9:00. Students circulate to find a different partner for each time, recording those pairings to use later when a specific one is called.

To keep this strategy effective, I regularly reset those partnerships rather than keeping them fixed for long periods of time. Each time we revisit clock partnering, I change the clock times and conditions so students are not always working with the same people. Sometimes I say, *"One of your partners must be taller than you,"* or *"Find someone who has more siblings than you,"* or *"Choose someone who is older than you."* These playful criteria not only spark conversations students might not otherwise have but also encourage them to see their classmates in new ways. By the end of the first month, students have interacted with nearly everyone in the room, breaking down barriers and building familiarity.

I use these partnerships for quick discussions, review activities, peer feedback, and even problem-solving tasks. When I say, *"Meet with your six o'clock partner,"* the room shifts into action within seconds. There is no wasted time deciding who to work with, no awkwardness about being left out, and no cliques dominating the dynamic. Most importantly, what students see is that I expect them to be able to collaborate with anyone in the room, and what they experience is the growing sense that they are part of a cohesive community.

The benefit is more than just efficient transitions. Students learn that our classroom is a place where everyone has value and everyone has a role to play. Over time, the comfort and trust built through these structured partnerships spill over into group work and class-wide discussions. By varying the conditions for selection, I subtly teach students that flexibility and openness to others are not optional in our community; they are essential.

While structured pairings help students connect widely, they also need systems for supporting one another when challenges arise. This is where **Three Before Me** comes in.

Three Before Me: Harnessing the Power of Peers

One of the simplest yet most effective strategies I use to foster collaboration is what I call **Three Before Me**. The rule is straightforward: before asking me for help, students must first seek assistance from three classmates. This builds a culture where the default is not "*ask the teacher*," but "*ask the community*." Students learn quickly that the classroom is full of resources beyond me, and often they discover solutions faster by checking with their peers.

The benefits go beyond efficiency. When students teach each other, their own understanding deepens, and the classroom becomes a network of shared expertise rather than a one-way street from me to them. It also keeps me from being pulled in ten different directions at once, especially during labs or collaborative activities.

I once observed a teacher, we will call her Sandra, who struggled without this strategy in place. She was trying to run a Chromebook-based lesson, and the content was challenging. Hands shot up across the room, and she rushed from desk to desk, tripping over backpacks, trying to respond. As she grew overwhelmed, students gave up and turned to their phones. By the end of class, most had not finished the assignment, not because they could not, but because the support they needed never reached them. Had a structure like **Three Before Me** been in place, students could have accessed help immediately from peers instead of waiting in frustration.

In my classroom, **Three Before Me** creates a powerful norm: learning is a collective effort. Additionally, students begin to see that their questions are valuable not only to themselves but to others, and they take pride in being the one who can explain or clarify for a peer. What might look like a small adjustment in practice actually transforms the classroom dynamic. Instead of me being the single bottleneck, every student becomes a resource, and the classroom begins to function as a true community of learners.

Of course, collaboration often extends beyond pairs. When we move into small groups or labs, structure becomes even more important. Without roles and clear placement, groups easily slide into imbalance or disorder. Intentional grouping strategies help prevent that.

Intentional Grouping Strategies: Structure Creates Accountability

In my classroom, active learning is the norm. Students are constantly engaged in labs, problem-solving activities, and collaborative projects. With so much movement and interaction, it is essential to build in structure so that the work does not dissolve into chaos. Two strategies that keep groups running smoothly are assigning roles and giving each group a specific location in the classroom.

Assigning Roles within Groups

When the plan is group work, I do not simply say, *"Get into groups and figure it out."* Without direction, one or two students will take over, others will disengage, and the learning will be uneven. To prevent this, I assign each student in the group a specific role, each with clear responsibilities that keep them accountable. These roles often include:

- **Materials Manager**: This student gathers all the supplies before the activity begins and ensures they are returned at the end. They check that everything is in working order and that nothing is missing. This role not only builds responsibility but also teaches students to value shared resources.

- **Lab Leader**: The leader is the group's point of contact with me. If I have additional tips, clarifications, or modifications, I share them with the leader, who then relays the information back to the group. This structure minimizes unnecessary noise and movement in the classroom and encourages the leader to develop communication and leadership skills.

- **Group Collaborator**: This student has the unique privilege of being able to move between groups. If the group is stuck, the collaborator checks in with other groups for inspiration or clarification utilizing the **Three Before Me** strategy. By design, this role fosters peer-to-peer learning and shows students that collaboration does not stop at the group level, but extends across the entire learning community.

- **Research Manager**: The researcher is responsible for consulting approved resources, whether it is textbooks, Chromebooks, or lab manuals, to support the group's work. This role helps prevent groups from spinning their wheels and keeps them grounded in accurate information.

- **Timekeeper**: Active learning activities often have multiple benchmarks or phases, and it is easy for groups to get bogged down on one step. The timekeeper monitors progress, announces time checks, and ensures that the group is moving toward completion within the given limits.

- **Cleanup Manager**: At the end of the activity, this student works with the materials manager to ensure supplies are returned, workspaces are clean, and the classroom is ready for the next group of students. Their job reinforces the expectation that we leave our space better than we found it.

By clearly defining these roles, every student knows exactly what their responsibility is. Hence, no one is allowed to sit back passively, and no one is burdened with carrying the entire group. The system also makes grading and accountability easier because students cannot claim they *"didn't know what to do."*

While these roles often take shape in my science classroom, particularly during labs and hands-on activities, the structure itself translates across content areas. A history teacher might adapt the materials manager into a document manager, or a language arts teacher might shift the research manager into a text analyst. The titles may change, but the purpose remains the same: every student has a defined responsibility that supports the group's success.

Assigning Group Locations in the Classroom

The physical placement of groups matters just as much as their roles. In my classroom, I assign each group a specific location. This structure keeps traffic patterns predictable, makes it easier for me to circulate, and ensures equitable access to materials.

The arrangement is also strategic. Groups with students who may need extra support, motivation, or redirection are placed closer to my workstation. Groups that work more independently can be placed farther away. This proximity allows me to offer help when it is most needed without hovering over everyone.

Assigning group locations signals that space is intentional. Just like routines and roles, where students sit and work becomes part of the structure that supports smooth learning. Over time, students come to understand that this structure exists to reduce distraction and uncertainty, allowing them to focus on doing their best work.

Once students are comfortable with small groups, I expand their collaboration into whole-class discussions. For example, seminars give students the chance to connect not only with their group but with the entire learning community.

Seminar Circles: Guiding Students into Meaningful Dialogue

A seminar discussion is a structured way for students to engage in meaningful dialogue around a shared text. Rather than simply answering questions or listening to a lecture, students gather together in a circle, share their reflections, and respond to one another's ideas. At its best, a seminar centers on building understanding through conversation rather than arriving at a single correct answer.

In my Anatomy and Physiology class, seminar took the form of biweekly book discussions. Every other Friday, we gathered into a circle and reflected on a chapter from *Brain Rules* by John Medina (2008). Students created their own reflection questions, and together we explored not only the science in the text but also how its ideas applied to learning. These days became what I called my warm and fuzzy Fridays because the discussions built such a strong sense of community. Students debated, challenged each other respectfully, and grew passionate about questions such as, *"If Medina is right about the brain, then why is school structured the way it is?"* For me, it was a dream scenario: students were reading deeply, thinking critically, and building relationships with one another through conversation.

Then COVID happened. When we returned, I discovered something I had taken for granted. Students no longer knew how to communicate naturally in this setting. Seminar transformed from engaging to awkward, even painful at times. I had told them what to do, I had modeled the behavior, and we had rehearsed it, but it still fell flat. Finally, not wanting to abandon seminar altogether, I found a YouTube video of students participating in a real seminar discussion. Watching peers their own age interact authentically gave my students the breakthrough they needed. They began to understand the flow of conversation and how to respond to one another without relying on me to guide every turn.

While admittedly post-COVID seminars never fully returned to the warm and fuzzy Fridays I remembered, they did improve significantly. That experience reinforced an important truth: we cannot assume students know how to communicate in academic discussions. Just as we teach routines for entering the classroom or handling supplies, we must also teach and model how to engage respectfully in dialogue. When we do, seminars can become powerful tools for both learning and community building.

After students experience the give-and-take of seminars, they are ready for the next step: presenting their own ideas. Small group presentations provide a bridge between informal discussion and formal public speaking.

Small Group Presentations: An Efficient Confidence Booster

Small group presentations are an alternative to the traditional model where every student presents in front of the entire class. Instead of asking thirty-two students to take turns speaking to a full audience, which can be overwhelming both in terms of time and anxiety, students are divided into groups of five or six. Within each group, students present to their peers only, which dramatically changes the experience.

Implementing small group presentations is straightforward. I divide the class into groups, assign or allow topics depending on the lesson, and provide a clear rubric. Each group listens attentively as individuals present, and they use the rubric to provide feedback. Because the audience is smaller and familiar, students feel more comfortable taking risks, and the process moves much more quickly. Presentations that might take multiple class periods and many hours via a whole-class setting can be completed in the time it would normally take for only a handful of students to present.

The benefits go far beyond saving time. Small group presentations help minimize the "public speaking freakout" many students experience, particularly those who struggle with confidence. Students are more willing to share their ideas when the pressure of facing the entire class is removed. At the same time, peers practice listening, providing constructive feedback, and learning from one another. With the help of a strong rubric, assessment becomes easier for me as well, since peers take an active role in evaluating presentations.

Ultimately, small group presentations preserve the essential skills of speaking and presenting while removing unnecessary barriers. They transform what could be a painful or intimidating process into one that builds confidence, supports peer learning, and uses time efficiently.

Eventually, collaboration moves into the high-stakes arena of larger group projects. Here, accountability is everything.

Group Projects: Fostering Fair and Equitable Collaboration

Group projects are one of the most challenging yet rewarding activities we can assign in the classroom. This is one of the few times that I allow students to choose their partners, but I remind them to choose wisely because their performance will reflect not only their group but their individual effort as well. To make sure accountability is built into the process, I require both self-assessments and peer-assessments. This ensures that students who contribute meaningfully are recognized, and those who fail to participate do not ride on the work of others. The grade is always a combination of the overall group grade and the student's individual contribution.

All work for these projects must be completed in Google tools so that every keystroke can be traced. This approach ensures fairness by providing a clear record of who worked, when they contributed, and how much they participated. When questions arise, there is no room for debate.

I once had a parent furious that his daughter received a zero for a group project. He insisted she had contributed and was only absent on presentation day. Peer assessments suggested otherwise, but without documentation the situation could have turned into a "he said, she said" exchange. Instead, I pulled up the Google history, which showed she had never accessed the shared documents. The conversation ended there. The following year, that same student retook the course, demonstrated maturity, and later thanked me for holding her accountable.

When structured this way, group projects become more than academic exercises. They are opportunities to teach fairness, honesty, and responsibility. Moreover, students learn that collaboration requires effort from everyone, and that their own contribution matters both to their peers and to their grade.

Peer-to-Peer Relations are Vital to a Cohesive Community

What unites all of these strategies is the message they send: collaboration is about community. By establishing clear norms, structuring group work with intentionality, and holding students accountable for both their contributions and their respect toward others, we create a classroom culture where learning is shared and strengthen through structured collaboration. In addition, these practices teach students that everyone has a role to play, and that success comes from trust, fairness, and responsibility.

That same spirit of collaboration must extend beyond the classroom walls as well. Just as students thrive when they know their peers will support them, teachers thrive when parents are part of the learning community. Building positive parent relationships is the natural next step in fostering a cohesive classroom pack.

Teacher-Parent Relationships: Expanding the Pack

For years, I was diligent about mass parent communication and reaching out when problems arose, but I rarely thought about intentionally building positive relationships with parents from the start. Earning my Ed.D. and some key classroom experiences changed my perspective.

Research confirms what experience showed me: the more parents trust the teacher, the better the student's behavior tends to be (Jones & Jones, 2021). Trust begins with connection. Early in the year, we can ask parents to share their goals for their child, their student's strengths and challenges, and any cultural or family information that will help us support learning. Even a short, positive call before an issue arises builds a reservoir of goodwill that we can draw on later.

When parents feel included in the classroom pack, they are more likely to partner with us when challenges come. Community is strongest when it extends beyond the classroom walls.

Research Spotlight: Structured Collaboration Raises the Bar

Structured collaboration, where group work is carefully designed with roles, clear goals, and accountability, has strong support from educational research. A meta-analysis by the Education Endowment Foundation (2021) found that collaborative or cooperative learning approaches in small groups of three to five students led, on average, to five additional months' progress over a school year compared to more traditional instruction. Similarly, Cornell University's Center for Teaching Innovation (n.d.) notes that when tasks in group work are well designed so that everyone has something to contribute and everyone's contribution matters, students develop not only content knowledge but also critical thinking, communication skills, leadership, and a stronger sense of responsibility. Research also shows that unstructured or loosely structured group work often fails to produce these benefits, as inequities emerge and some students disengage (Cohen, 1994). Structured collaboration, by contrast, provides scaffolding for interaction, models of discourse, and norms for accountability, all of which lead to higher engagement and deeper learning (Hirschy & Wilson, 2023).

Practical Pack-Building Strategies

The first month of school is the pack building phase. This is when routines expand into relationships and the structures of community begin to take shape. Just as puppies in training learn to settle into the rhythm of a pack, students learn how to interact productively with peers, respect roles, and contribute to the whole. Here are some strategies that help turn a collection of individuals into a cohesive classroom community:

1. **Set Collaborative Norms Early**
   Avoid assuming students know what collaboration looks like. Model and define the difference between helping and copying, between listening respectfully and dismissing ideas. Clear expectations ensures that group work is productive rather than frustrating.

2. **Rotate Partners with Purpose**
   Clock partnering ensures that students connect with many peers instead of clinging to the same few. Creative criteria for partners, such as height, siblings, or hobbies, keep the process fresh and fun while also building flexibility.

3. **Make Peers the First Resource**
   Three Before Me trains students to rely on each other instead of waiting for the teacher to swoop in. This not only lightens our load but also builds confidence and accountability within the group.

4. **Assign Roles and Locations**
   Give every group member a defined responsibility and a clear place to work. Roles like materials manager, timekeeper, and collaborator prevent freeloading, while designated group spaces help us circulate and support students efficiently.

5. **Teach Dialogue, Not Just Content**
   Seminar discussions and small group presentations push students beyond surface answers. These activities teach them how to speak,

listen, and build on each other's ideas. The process is as valuable as the content itself.

6. **Build Accountability into Group Projects**
   Pair group grades with self and peer-assessments so that effort and responsibility are distributed fairly. Additionally, use digital tools to track contributions, making the process transparent for both students and parents.

Each of these strategies is more than a technique; together they form the patterns of a pack. They signal that everyone has a role, everyone has a voice, and everyone is responsible for the community we are building.

Closing Reflection

Building a cohesive classroom community depends on rhythm, structure, and intention. Just as a pack draws strength from unity, classrooms thrive when trust is nurtured in every direction. Teacher and student relationships grow when expectations are held with care, showing students that consistency and respect work together. Relationships among students strengthen through structured collaboration, where clear norms, intentional roles, and shared responsibility turn groups into communities. Partnerships with families flourish when that same trust extends outward through communication and mutual respect.

Together, these relationships create the harmony of a learning pack that extends beyond the classroom. When roles are clear, respect is mutual, and support flows among students, teachers, and families, learning takes place within a safe and cohesive community. In that space, students are free to take risks, support one another, and grow not only as learners, but as people who understand the power of belonging.

Reflection Questions

1. When students test boundaries in the first month, how do you respond in ways that build respect?
2. What collaborative norms are most important for your classroom, and how do you make sure students understand the difference between real collaboration and simple convenience?

3. Which grouping strategies have worked best in your own teaching, and how might intentional roles or locations improve accountability?
4. How do you ensure that every student feels included and valued in peer-to-peer activities, even when they are not naturally outgoing or confident?
5. What steps can you take early in the year to build trust with parents so they see you as a partner in supporting their child's learning and behavior?

Try This Tomorrow

Peer Accountability in Action

- Identify one activity in which students often rely heavily on you for support.
- Introduce the **Three Before Me** rule and explain that students must check with three classmates before approaching you.
- Observe how the flow of the classroom changes when students look to one another first.
- At the end of class, debrief briefly with students about how this felt and what they learned from helping and being helped.

Chapter 4: Pavlov's Pup – The Psychology Behind Classroom Management

At this point, you may be wondering: why are the students complying? What magic trick have I not revealed yet? The truth is that there is no magic—no smoke and mirrors. Everything I have shared comes straight from principles of behavioral psychology.

Behavioral psychology illustrates that both human and canine behavior are learned actions shaped by consequences. If the consequence is pleasant, the behavior is likely to increase. If it is unpleasant, the behavior is likely to decrease. That pattern holds true whether you are training a puppy not to chew shoes or teaching a teenager to put their phone away when class begins.

The ABCs of Behavior

Learned behavior typically follows a predictable pattern:

- **Antecedent**: what happens right before the behavior.
- **Behavior**: the observable action.
- **Consequence**: what follows the behavior.

The power lies in the consequence. When we understand this sequence, we can adjust the consequence to influence what happens next. For example, if a student talks out of turn, the consequence we give, attention, redirection, or silence, will determine whether that behavior is more or less likely to happen again.

Reinforcement: The Fuel for Habits

Reinforcement is about strengthening desired behaviors. It is the steady fuel that keeps routines alive long after the novelty of the first few weeks has worn off. The distinction between positive and negative reinforcement often confuses people, but in practice both are straightforward.

Positive Reinforcement means adding something desirable to increase a behavior. In the classroom, this can be as simple as a nonverbal cue such as a smile, a nod, a thumbs up, or even an "air high five" across the room. These small signals communicate recognition without disrupting the flow of a lesson. Tangible tools like **Thank You Slips** give students visible acknowledgment that their effort is noticed. Privileges also carry weight: letting a table group be first to grab backpacks, assigning special classroom jobs, or allowing students to help set up materials. Social rewards are also powerful: chatting with a student about their weekend game, sending a positive email home, or letting the class vote on a music playlist to enjoy during work time. What matters is that reinforcement feels genuine and is tied directly to the desired behavior. Over time, students learn that meeting expectations consistently earns attention, trust, and privileges.

Negative Reinforcement means removing something unpleasant once the desired behavior occurs. This is often overlooked, but it is just as effective in shaping habits. For example, I might let a timer continue beeping until all students are seated and attentive; the sound disappears as soon as compliance happens. Sometimes I simply pause mid-sentence and wait silently until every student has eyes on me, resuming only once I have full attention. A slight frown, steady eye contact, or hand gesture can act as subtle prompts that create temporary discomfort, which vanishes the moment students correct themselves. These cues are not punishments, but reminders. The "relief" of the discomfort is the reinforcement. Students quickly learn that when they meet expectations, the annoyance (or pressure) is lifted and class continues smoothly.

Together, positive and negative reinforcement form the backbone of classroom management. The aim is clarity, helping students connect their choices with the responses that follow. Early on, reinforcement is most effective when it is frequent and visible, allowing students to clearly see which behaviors lead to positive outcomes. As those behaviors become established, reinforcement can be delivered less often. At this stage, variability becomes important. When reinforcement is not guaranteed or predictable, behaviors tend to strengthen and persist over time.

The Gambling Theory of Reinforcement

One of the most fascinating principles of behavioral psychology is the concept of *intermittent reinforcement*, often called the gambling theory. At its core, the idea is simple: behaviors that are rewarded occasionally, and without a predictable pattern, become some of the hardest to extinguish.

Think about slot machines. If gamblers won every single time they pulled the lever, the excitement would disappear, and casinos would go broke. If they never won, they would stop playing. What keeps them coming back is the unpredictability. The occasional payout, even if it is small, is powerful enough to keep the behavior going far longer than consistent reinforcement ever would.

In classrooms, the same principle applies. When we are deliberate, students learn that certain behaviors (raising their hand, completing work on time, showing respect) will reliably result in reinforcement, whether that reinforcement is praise, a **Thank You Slip**, or another form of recognition. Once the behavior becomes established, though, we can fade the reinforcement, providing it less often, at irregular intervals. Students never know exactly when the reinforcement will occur, which keeps the behavior alive and strong.

For example, in the first few weeks I might hand out **Thank You Slips** frequently, making sure students clearly connect the behavior with the reward. But by the second or third month, I may only hand out slips occasionally. The student whose phone is parked and eyes on me may not be recognized every time, but when they are, it feels significant. The unpredictability keeps the behavior consistent without requiring me to reinforce constantly.

This is the brilliance of intermittent reinforcement: it builds habits that last. However, there is a caution here. If we inadvertently reinforce undesirable behavior intermittently, we can cement it just as powerfully. The student who blurts out answers, for instance, and only occasionally gets attention from it, may actually be harder to redirect than the student who always gets ignored. The occasional "payout," such as a laugh from peers, a nod from the teacher, or even an accidental smile, is enough to keep them trying.

That is exactly what happened with Adam in Chapter 1. His witty interruptions earned attention from me on the first day, but then not again. That unpredictability, the chance that his humor might land and get a reaction, was all it took to strengthen the very behavior I was trying to curb. Without realizing it, I had made his interruptions function like a slot machine: keep trying, and maybe you will hit the jackpot of attention.

The lesson for us is twofold. First, we must be generous and consistent with reinforcement at the beginning, so students learn clearly which behaviors matter. Then, as habits form, we can taper to intermittent reinforcement, creating behaviors that are durable and self-sustaining. Second, we must be vigilant not to accidentally give even the smallest reinforcement to behaviors we do not want, because those are the ones students will keep testing, just like gamblers pulling the lever one more time.

Research Spotlight: The Science of Intermittent Reinforcement

Behavioral and psychological research has long shown that how reinforcement is delivered matters just as much as what is being reinforced. Studies of reinforcement schedules demonstrate that after a behavior is established through regular reward, switching to a less predictable, intermittent schedule helps sustain the behavior longer. For example, in school settings, variable-interval schedules, where rewards are given at unpredictable times, encourage steady participation and reduce the chance that students will "give up" when rewards aren't immediate (Lee & Belfiore, 1997; Hulac et al., 2016).

These findings are similar to what is seen in gambling research: people keep trying because of the chance of a reward. In classrooms, this means that reinforcement applied thoughtfully (not constantly, but with enough regularity and unpredictability) builds habits, attention, and behavior that withstand the normal ups and downs of the school year.

Punishment: A Tool to Use Sparingly

While reinforcement builds, punishment attempts to stop behavior. The problem is that punishment often creates stress, damages relationships, and fails to produce predictable improvements. That is why it should never be the centerpiece of classroom management. When necessary, we use it with care, as a last resort, and in the least harmful form possible.

- **Positive Punishment**: Adding something unpleasant to decrease a behavior. For example, if students repeatedly talk over directions, I might stop the lesson, reset the timer, and require everyone to practice the listening routine again before moving forward. The added inconvenience is unpleasant enough to discourage the disruption, yet it is minimal in long-term impact and framed as practice rather than punishment. The goal is not humiliation but a reminder that procedures matter.

- **Negative Punishment**: Taking away something desirable to decrease a behavior. For example, requiring a student to place their phone in a pencil bag for the rest of class. This is the only form of punishment I consistently use throughout the school year. Phones present a unique challenge: there is very little in standards-aligned lessons more enticing to a teenager than what their device has to offer. Just as in dog training, where you must provide something more pleasurable to redirect an unwanted behavior, students' phones are often too reinforcing to compete with through academic tasks alone. In these cases, removal becomes not only the most effective option but sometimes the only one, which helps explain why more and more states are banning phones in classrooms.

Sometimes punishment can be flipped into reinforcement. For instance, instead of calling out a student for being off-task, I might walk over and hand a **Thank You Slip** to the student sitting right next to them who is working diligently. The message spreads without confrontation: attention flows towards the desirable behavior instead of the undesirable one.

Doggy See, Doggy Do

When we adopted Liberty, a five-year-old, 140-pound Great Dane, we discovered she had never had her toenails clipped. I tried the recommended desensitization techniques—introducing the clippers, touching her toes, pairing it all with high-value treats. Progress came slowly, but when I finally clipped one nail, Liberty declared, *"Absolutely not!"*

Then there was Bella, our other Dane, who had grown up with toenail trims as a normal, treat-filled ritual. Bella would race to her spot, cross her paws, and wait eagerly for her pedicure. One day, I shut Liberty on the other side of a glass door so I could trim Bella's nails without interference. Liberty stood transfixed, drooling on the glass, watching Bella get clip after clip, treat after treat. When I opened the door, Liberty bounded over, flopped down, crossed her paws, and let me trim every nail.

It was a classic case of monkey see, monkey do, or in this case, doggy see, doggy do. She saw the behavior I wanted modeled and rewarded, and she wanted the same outcome. A similar pattern unfolds in classrooms. When we recognize students who are on-task right next to those who are not, the off-task students quickly realize where the attention and rewards are flowing. Reinforcing the right behavior, even indirectly, can redirect the wrong behavior without confrontation.

Hyperawareness: The Teacher's Superpower

All of this only works if we notice what is happening in the first place. Jacob Kounin (1970) called it *with-it-ness*; I call it hyperawareness. Effective teachers see all, hear all, and anticipate where problems might arise before they fully develop. We notice the student quietly packing up early, the pair of friends whispering a little too much, or the subtle shift in body language that signals disengagement.

Hyperawareness is an elevated level of intentional presence. It comes from carefully structuring the room so we can see every student, moving constantly so students never know when we will be at their elbow, and reinforcing the behaviors we want more of. Like a parent with "eyes in the back of their head," we cultivate an environment where students learn that nothing escapes our attention. This vigilance, paired with calm consistency, prevents small sparks from becoming wildfires and keeps the focus where it belongs: on learning.

Practical Behavioral Psychology Strategies

Understanding the psychology behind behavior allows classroom routines to run more smoothly and prevents many problems before they start. These strategies draw on principles of conditioning and reinforcement to support a calm, focused learning environment.

1. **Reinforce Early and Often**
   At the start, make recognition visible and frequent. Smile, nod, hand out **Thank You Slips**, or give small privileges to students meeting expectations. As routines solidify, shift to intermittent reinforcement to keep behaviors strong, just like a slot machine keeps players engaged.

2. **Use Negative Reinforcement Wisely**
   If an unpleasant stimulus (like a timer beep or a pause in instruction) is motivating students to comply, remove it immediately when the desired behavior occurs. The relief teaches students that their cooperation restores calm and flow.

3. **Avoid Overusing Punishment**
   Punishment may stop a behavior in the moment, but it does not teach the desired replacement behavior. Use it sparingly, keep it minimal, and when possible, flip it into reinforcement, such as rewarding the students sitting near the one off-task.

4. **Recognize the Power of Modeling**
   Students are always watching. Just as Bella taught Liberty through example, reinforcing the students closest to the problem-behavior often inspires the others to follow suit. In this way, monkey see, monkey do becomes an instructional tool rather than a cliché.

5. **Practice Hyperawareness**
   Develop a high level of awareness by circulating steadily, keeping every student in view, and reinforcing desirable behaviors.

Closing Reflection

By the time we reach the end of the first month, routines are established, expectations are firm, and the class is running via predictable patterns. This is not magic; it is design. Through reinforcement, careful use of consequences, and ever-present hyperawareness, we build a classroom where students understand that their behavior has meaning and impact.

Reinforcement teaches them what earns attention, while sparing use of punishment ensures that dignity is preserved. Modeling, consistency, and presence make it clear that the classroom is a safe place where effort is noticed and success is possible. Just as Liberty learned to follow Bella's example, students learn by watching the responses of those around them. In this way, the classroom community becomes self-sustaining.

As we transition from this focus on behavior to the deeper work of building authentic relationships, one truth remains: structure is about trust.

And trust is the foundation on which everything else in the classroom will rest.

Reflection Questions

1. Think of a time when you accidentally reinforced an undesirable behavior, as I did with Adam. How could you have shifted to reinforcing the students showing the behavior you *did* want?
2. Which reinforcers (both positive and negative) already exist in your classroom, and how might you use them more intentionally?
3. What is one behavior that you currently punish that could instead be reshaped with reinforcement?
4. How consistent is your reinforcement schedule? Describe what your reinforcement looks like in practice and explain how it impacts student engagement.
5. What adjustments could you make in your classroom setup or movement patterns to strengthen your own hyperawareness?

Try This Tomorrow

Reinforcement Inventory

- Before your next class, list the reinforcers you use most often, such as smiles, thumbs up, **Thank You Slips**, first book bag retrieval, or music when appropriate.
- During class, intentionally use at least three different reinforcers and deliver them immediately.
- After class, note which reinforcers were most effective and consider how to build them into your regular practice.

Part 2: Love 'Em to Learn 'Em

The best advice I ever received as a preservice teacher came from a beloved middle school social studies teacher named Augie. He told me, *"You have to love 'em to learn 'em."* His meaning was simple and profound: if we do not truly care about our students first, they will never fully learn from us. Those words shaped not only how I entered the profession, but how I have lived it.

I remember sitting in my first interview and being handed three words: *relationship, rigor, relevance.* I was asked to rank them and explain my reasoning. With Augie's advice echoing in my mind, I chose relationship first, relevance second, and rigor third. I explained that without a foundation of trust and care, relevance would not matter, and rigor would never land. Within hours, I was hired. That order has guided me ever since, through the days of masked teaching during COVID, through classroom highs and lows, and through the countless students who reminded me that relationship always comes first.

If Part 1 established the *rules* of the game through the boundaries, routines, and structure, Part 2 turns toward the *heart* of the game. Once students know the rules, they need to know they belong, and most importantly, they need to know we care. They need to feel seen, encouraged, inspired, and motivated to grow. That is where the work of relationship and connection comes in.

The chapters ahead explore the dimensions of this work:

- **Pack Bonds – Relationships, Relationships, Relationships**
- **Paws and Potential – Cultivating a Learning Mindset**
- **Puppy Voice – Enthusiasm is Contagious**
- **Chasing Motivation – Activating What Drives Students to Learn**

Together, these chapters remind us that teaching extends beyond content. Connection comes first. Love them first, and the learning will follow.

Chapter 5: Pack Bonds – Relationships, Relationships, Relationships

When Bella was delivered to our home late one evening, we had only ever seen her online. Knowing she was a Great Dane, we pictured a massive puppy bounding through the door. What arrived instead was a chihuahua-sized body with paws and ears so oversized she looked like she had been assembled from the wrong parts box. At just 8 weeks old, Bella was awkward and irresistibly adorable. She made us laugh every time she bounded about, tripping over her paws, her body not yet sure how to manage all that she would one day grow into.

It was tempting to simply indulge her sweetness, letting her antics slide because she was so small and endearing. But love for Bella meant guiding her with routines, setting gentle boundaries, and providing the structure that would help her grow into the gentle giant we knew she would become. Puppies grow, and what feels cute in the moment becomes much harder to manage later if the foundation isn't laid with care.

A similar pull shows up in our classrooms. At the beginning of the year, it is tempting to relax boundaries because we want students to like us. But genuine relationships are not built on permissiveness; they are built on trust. Just like with Bella, what students need most is the assurance that expectations are steady, that respect is mutual, and that they are cared for within a safe structure.

The solution is the same for both puppies and students: structure and consistency that spring from care. What sustains relationships is not the grand gestures or the initial charm but steady routines, clear expectations, and the reassurance of belonging. The routines we established in the first month laid the foundation; now we build upon them with relationship maintenance that is intentional, consistent, and deeply rooted in care.

Meeting Needs Before Meeting Standards

During COVID, when masks covered every face, I realized how much I relied on expressions to read emotions. That is when the emoji name plates were born. What began as a practical solution to missing visual cues soon became one of the most powerful relationship-building practices of my career. Maslow's (1943) hierarchy of needs explains why. His model illustrates that before higher-order learning can happen, students' basic needs must be met: safety, belonging, recognition, and care. Only when those foundations are secure can students climb toward confidence, creativity, and deep learning.

In practice, the emojis became more than symbols. They were daily invitations to connect. A sad face prompted a quiet check-in, a silly face often sparked laughter, and sometimes I gave students prompts such as *"show me your favorite photo,"* whether of a pet, a best friend, or a cherished place on Earth. These conversations were not small talk; they were intentional relationship maintenance built into my curriculum.

Through these moments, students learned that I cared about who they were, not just what they produced. The emojis opened doors to conversations that revealed the emotional realities they carried with them each day. And once those needs were acknowledged, trust grew. Meeting needs before meeting standards is not about lowering expectations, it is about honoring the order in which people thrive. When students' emotional worlds are seen, their capacity for learning expands. If we take care of the person, the brain will follow. One of the simplest ways to do that is by using their names.

Power of a Name

One of the most powerful tools we have is using students' names. Think about it: in a noisy room, if someone says your name, your attention snaps back immediately. Names cut through distraction and send the message that you are known.

Early in the year, I work hard to learn names quickly, and I keep using them even after I know them by heart. Saying *"Thank you, Jasmine, for getting started right away"* or *"Daniel, I appreciate how you helped your partner"* reinforces both behavior and belonging. Students lean in when they hear their name. They feel seen. Just like puppies respond to hearing their name during training, students respond when we show that their identity matters.

Eye Contact: Small Act, Big Impact

Eye contact is equally powerful. In fact, psychologists call it a social glue. Looking a student in the eye when giving directions, offering praise, or checking in communicates more than words ever could. It says, *"I see you, and you matter here."*

This is where I sometimes, once again, think about my Great Dane, Bella. She has a habit of seeking me out and staring deeply into my eyes when she wants affection. I tease her by saying, *"Bella, you just need your oxytocin fix."* And in truth, she does. Research shows that mutual eye contact between humans and dogs actually increases oxytocin, the bonding hormone, for both (Nagasawa et al., 2015). Similar effects have been observed in humans, where oxytocin is associated with increased attention to the eye region during social interaction (Guastella et al., 2008). When I look my students in the eye, even briefly, that moment of shared attention strengthens our relationship. Moreover, it helps create the trust and safety that learning requires.

A Tail Wag to SEL

I want to pause here to acknowledge the growing emphasis on social-emotional learning (SEL), the focus on students' emotional well-being and relationships. It is a critical field, and I fully support the recognition that students' emotional needs matter in classrooms. At the same time, I know that many excellent books and programs already cover SEL in depth. My goal here is not to add another program to the mix but to highlight the everyday, human practices that make a difference. Using names, making eye contact, and showing consistent care are small acts that have big impact. They are classroom management at its core: building authentic relationships where students feel secure enough to learn.

Research Spotlight: The Power of Relationships

Research consistently shows that authentic teacher–student relationships improve not only classroom behavior but also academic achievement. John Hattie's (2008) *Visible Learning* identifies teacher–student relationships as one of the most influential factors in student success, highlighting that the connection between teacher and student can make a meaningful difference in learning outcomes. Similarly, Pianta et al. (2012) found that when students feel connected to their teachers, they demonstrate greater engagement, better self-regulation, and improved academic outcomes. The message is clear: authentic relationships are not "extra." They are essential.

Respect as the Cornerstone

If there is one thing students crave more than being liked, it is being respected. Respect is the foundation of authentic connection.

Teenagers are still developing empathy. The prefrontal cortex, which governs self-control and perspective-taking, does not fully mature until a person is in their mid-twenties. This means teenagers may not always show understanding of others' feelings in the moment. But what they do understand deeply is fairness. When we treat them with dignity, even when addressing misbehavior, they recognize it as fairness, and eventually mirror it back.

I once had a student who disliked me no matter how much effort I put into connecting. Later I learned I resembled someone who had hurt her family, and she carried that association into our relationship. That experience reminded me: not every student will like us, no matter how hard we try, but every student can respect us.

Respect means preserving student dignity, even when they push boundaries. For instance, I never call out grumbles, eye rolls, or backtalk in front of peers. Instead, I pull the student aside privately and inquire, *"I do not treat you that way, so shouldn't I receive the same respect in return?"* The tone is calm, firm, and fair. The conversation is not about humiliation; it is about modeling self-control and reinforcing mutual respect.

When we preserve dignity, hold students accountable with fairness, and model respectful behavior ourselves, we send a message that reverberates throughout the classroom culture: this is a place where every person matters.

Fostering Peer Respect

Respect cannot stop with teacher-student interactions; it must permeate the classroom community. Students spend much of their day together, and how they treat one another sets the tone for learning. My classroom is a "peace and love" environment, where cliques and social hierarchies are left at the door.

From the first month onward, I reinforce that students do not have to be friends, but they do have to treat one another with kindness, compassion, and dignity. I explain that learning is inherently vulnerable. When we attempt something difficult, we risk making mistakes. Students are more likely to take those risks if they know their peers will treat them with respect rather than ridicule.

To build that trust, I regularly create opportunities for students to interact with classmates they might not naturally choose. Some days I randomize partners. Other days I use lighthearted prompts like, *"Find a partner who shares your favorite color,"* or *"Work with someone who has a different birthday month."* Over time, these experiences communicate that every person in the room has value and that learning expands when we connect beyond familiar circles. With continued practice, students grow more comfortable stepping outside their social groups and come to see the classroom as a community where everyone belongs.

When respect becomes part of the cultural fabric, students start holding one another to that standard. They learn that our classroom thrives when every member feels seen, heard, and supported.

Building Bridges Beyond the Classroom

Relationships are not limited to the walls of the classroom. Parents and guardians play a powerful role in shaping how students approach school. When we build strong partnerships with families, students benefit from a unified network of support.

One of the most impactful practices I adopted was sending five positive emails to parents each week. These notes were short and specific: *"Your son was a fantastic lab partner today! He helped his group stay organized and made sure everyone contributed."* Many parents told me it was the first positive comment they had ever received from a teacher, even after years of schooling. In one case, a mother was moved to tears, explaining that her junior in high school had never had a teacher speak about him so positively. That student's behavior remained stellar for the entire year, largely because he knew his teacher and his parent were aligned in believing in him.

I also send proactive messages before major tests or projects. These are not reminders in a punitive tone but celebrations of the work students have done: *"Your daughter has been working so diligently on her research project. Ask her to show you her notes. I think she would be proud to share them."* These kinds of updates invite parents into the learning process and equip them to support their children in ways that feel positive rather than stressful.

When parents see that I value their children and communicate openly, trust develops. And when parents trust teachers, research shows that student behavior and academic outcomes improve (Henderson & Mapp, 2002). Building bridges with families is a critical part of creating an environment where students thrive.

Practical Strategies for Lasting Relationships

Building authentic relationships requires intention and consistency. Here are strategies that keep relationships strong long after the first month of school has passed:

1. **Maintain One-on-One Connections**
   Continue daily or weekly check-ins, even if brief. For instance, a quick acknowledgment of a student's effort, mood, or interests reinforces that they are still seen and valued.

2. **Use Names and Eye Contact Intentionally**
   Calling students by name communicates belonging and recognition. Pairing it with eye contact shows presence and respect. A simple, *"Thank you, Jordan, for jumping right in,"* said while making eye contact, has far more impact than generic praise. These small moments build trust and let students know they matter.

3. **Model and Reinforce Peer Respect**
   Explicitly recognize students who treat peers kindly during vulnerable moments. For example, a simple *"I appreciate how you listened without interrupting"* reinforces the culture of respect.

4. **Send Positive Parent Notes Regularly**
   Do not wait for problems. Establish the pattern of sharing success so that if a concern ever arises, parents already know you care.

5. **Preserve Student Dignity**
   Address misbehavior calmly and privately. The goal is correction, not humiliation. Students remember how we handle them in their lowest moments, and dignity preserved is trust maintained.

6. **Balance Structure with Care**
   Keep routines predictable while making room for student voice and choice. Reliability builds trust, while flexibility communicates respect for individuality.

Relationships are not built in a single act of kindness, a single week of effort, or even a month of consistent routines. They grow through intentional, repeated actions that quietly affirm to students and parents: I care. You matter. You belong.

Closing Reflection

Relationships are not a box to check during the first month of school and then set aside; they are like raising a puppy, built day by day through steady care, patience, and attention. They require us to show up consistently, notice when extra support is needed, and celebrate even the smallest wins along the way. When we invest in relationships with students, we create a classroom where respect, safety, and trust allow learning to flourish.

These relationships are strengthened by the ordinary rhythms of class. Calling a student by name, pausing for eye contact, or offering a quiet check-in are not distractions from the curriculum, they are the curriculum of care that makes academic learning possible. When relationship maintenance is woven into daily practice, students experience stability, belonging, and a foundation strong enough to support rigorous learning.

Authentic relationships are the core of teaching. Without them, even the best curriculum in the world cannot find its footing. With them, even the most reluctant learners can settle in and become part of the classroom pack.

Reflection Questions

1. How do you currently build authentic relationships with students beyond academics? Where could you be more intentional?
2. In what ways do you invite students to feel safe enough to be vulnerable in their learning?
3. How do you currently engage parents or guardians in positive communication? What new practices could strengthen that connection?
4. What habits or rituals could you establish to maintain relationship-building all year long, even during the busiest seasons?

Try This Tomorrow

One Authentic Connection

- Greet every student at some point during class using their name and eye contact.
- Add one personal question or comment, such as *"Good morning, Jordan, how was your soccer game last night?"* or *"Hi, Maya, I saw that new book you're reading, what do you think so far?"*
- Notice how this small, consistent action reinforces that students are known, valued, and seen.
- Reflect on how one authentic connection at a time builds trust and loyalty within the classroom pack.

Chapter 6: Paws and Potential – Cultivating a Learning Mindset

When Liberty joined our family, she was already five years old. Unlike Bella, who had grown up with us, Liberty came with her own history, habits, and fears. One of the biggest was the staircase. To Liberty, those steps might as well have been a mountain. She would plant herself firmly at the bottom, her whole-body tense with uncertainty. It was not that she was unwilling; it was that the task seemed impossible.

Teaching Liberty to climb those stairs was not just about the physical act of moving upward. It was about shaping her mindset. If she believed she could only succeed when things were easy or familiar, she would have stayed frozen at the bottom forever. But with patience, encouragement, and persistence, she tested one paw, then another. Slowly, she began to see that she could do more than she thought. Before long, Liberty was climbing the staircase with confidence.

Likewise, students face their own staircases every day. Speaking up in class, tackling a difficult assignment, or trying a new way of learning can feel just as intimidating as Liberty staring up at those steps. The way forward is a **Learning Mindset**. It is the belief that, *"I can do this. With effort, perseverance, and support, I can grow."* When students approach challenges this way, fear gives way to confidence, and each step becomes proof that they are capable of more than they imagined. This is the essence of mindset, and no one brought it into the educational conversation more prominently than Carol Dweck.

Mindset Unleashed: Dweck's Promise of Growth

Carol Dweck's *Mindset: The New Psychology of Success* (2006) captured the attention of schools across the country because it offered a simple and compelling idea: the way students think about their abilities shapes how they respond to challenges. She described two broad patterns of belief. A fixed mindset sees abilities as carved in stone, while a growth mindset sees them as qualities that can expand through effort, strategy, and support.

A fixed mindset frames qualities as predetermined. In other words, students who hold this belief see ability as something you either have or you do not.

When they fail, they interpret the failure as evidence of personal inadequacy rather than as feedback. Instead of seeing effort as a pathway to improvement, they often see it as proof of weakness. If you were really smart, they reason, you would not need to try so hard. As a result, these students avoid risk, shy away from challenge, and look for ways to protect the image of being capable rather than expose the possibility of struggle. Failure, to them, is not an event, it is an identity: *I am a failure.*

A growth mindset offers a very different lens. Here, ability is seen as expandable. Thus, students with this mindset recognize that effort, strategy, and support from others can build capacity. For them, failure may sting, but it does not define. Instead, it becomes information they can use to grow stronger. They lean into challenge, not because it feels easy, but because it promises growth. In this mindset, effort is not a sign of deficiency but a sign of investment.

The contrast between these two beliefs is striking, especially when translated into the daily realities of school. In one of Dweck's studies, seventh graders who held a growth mindset and earned poor grades on a test said they would study harder for the next one. Students with a fixed mindset, however, reported that they would study less or even consider cheating, convinced they simply did not "have it" for the subject (Dweck, 2006). The same event, failure, pushed one group to take responsibility and try again, and led the other to give up or deflect.

It is not hard to see why schools embraced this idea so quickly. Growth mindset felt hopeful, actionable, and deeply aligned with what educators wanted for their students. Indeed, if we could help learners believe they could improve, then challenges would transform into opportunities, and perseverance would replace avoidance. The message was simple: with the right mindset, students could take responsibility for their learning and behavior. Yet simplicity has its dangers. When complex ideas are boiled down too far, they risk becoming the very labels they set out to dismantle. That was true for mindset, and it was equally true for Howard Gardner's (1983) theory of multiple intelligences, which was also widely embraced but frequently oversimplified.

The Promise and Pitfall of Multiple Intelligences

Gardner's *Frames of Mind* (1983) introduced the theory of multiple intelligences and quickly swept through education. His framework broadened the definition of intelligence by placing musical, spatial, bodily-kinesthetic, interpersonal, and intrapersonal abilities alongside the traditional linguistic and logical-mathematical ones. For teachers, this felt revolutionary. Further, it validated what they already sensed in their classrooms: that intelligence was not one-size-fits-all and that students could excel in ways that traditional tests often overlooked.

The appeal was obvious. Gardner's model gave teachers a language for recognizing diverse strengths. For instance, a student who struggled with reading but excelled in art could now be celebrated for spatial intelligence. Furthermore, a child who organized playground games could be recognized for interpersonal intelligence. In an era dominated by standardized testing and narrow definitions of achievement, multiple intelligences felt hopeful and liberating.

Yet the very simplicity that made it appealing also made it vulnerable to distortion. In practice, Gardner's nuanced theory was often simplified into the more familiar framework of "learning styles." Schools and professional development programs collapsed intelligences into categories like visual, auditory, and kinesthetic. Students were asked to identify their "style," and teachers were encouraged to match instruction to those preferences.

The intention was positive, but the result was problematic because students began to use these categories as limits rather than strengths. For example, a student who believed she was a "hands-on learner" might refuse to engage in a reading task, insisting it was not her way of learning. Another who identified as a "visual learner" might tune out of a lecture entirely, convinced he could not learn without diagrams. Instead of empowering students, the conflation gave them permission to disengage and shift responsibility away from themselves and onto the teacher.

The irony is that Gardner himself has repeatedly clarified that multiple intelligences is not the same thing as learning styles, and he has warned against this exact misinterpretation (Strauss, 2013). But by the time the idea filtered through teacher workshops, textbooks, and curriculum guides, the nuance was often lost. What remained was a simplified model that, much like a fixed mindset, locked students into rigid categories.

The Shared Problem: Labels That Cage Us

Here is where the two theories unexpectedly meet. Dweck cautioned against a fixed mindset, yet when paired with Gardner's multiple intelligences, students' thinking often hardened into oversimplified learning-style labels. In both cases, frameworks meant to expand possibility ended up caging students in, diminishing the fluid nature of learning and, paradoxically, reinforcing the very fixedness Dweck warned against.

Labels carry weight. Once students adopt them, they become explanations, quietly turning into beliefs that guide how students define themselves. *"I am just not good at math." "I cannot learn this way." "I will never understand science."* These beliefs may sound harmless at first, but they often open the door to disengagement, low effort, or disruptive behavior. Instead of saying, "*I need to try harder,"* a student says, "*The teacher is not teaching the way I learn."* Responsibility shifts away from persistence and onto the educator's method.

The issue is that both Dweck's and Gardner's frameworks were often interpreted as static categories when, in reality, human development is rarely static. Dweck herself acknowledged that it is not simply nature or nurture, not genes or environment, but a constant interplay between the two (2006). Yet when her ideas filtered into classrooms, many students were told they were "fixed" or "growth," as if mindset was a permanent trait rather than a shifting state. Gardner faced the same problem: a model designed to expand our definition of intelligence ended up boxing students into narrow "styles" that were treated as unchanging identities.

Researchers have echoed this concern. Li and Bates (2019) found little evidence that mindset interventions reliably improve achievement, concluding that the relationship between mindset and outcomes is more complex than a fixed-versus-growth divide. Similarly, Pashler and colleagues (2008) found no credible evidence that tailoring instruction to learning styles improves outcomes, and Newton (2015) described learning styles as one of education's most persistent neuromyths. As previously noted, even Gardner himself has repeatedly clarified that multiple intelligences are not the same as learning styles, warning against this misinterpretation (Strauss, 2013).

The last few decades of psychology and neuroscience have repeatedly shown that human traits are not either/or. For instance, autism is now understood as a spectrum, not a single category. Further, gender identity, once framed as rigid, is now recognized as fluid for many individuals. Even the long-standing debate about nature versus nurture has given way to a more nuanced understanding that genes and environment are always in dynamic interaction. Why, then, would we assume that mindsets about learning are fixed categories?

Mindset is fluid. A student may feel confident and resilient in history class, only to shut down completely in math. Another may persist in athletics but avoid challenge in writing. Additionally, mindsets can even shift within a single class period: a student may begin a task with optimism, become discouraged at the first mistake, and recover with encouragement. To present students as either "fixed" or "growth" ignores the reality that mindset fluctuates constantly in response to context, support, and experience.

This matters for behavior. A student who believes *"I am bad at math"* may withdraw from the task, but that same student might eagerly persist when given a creative art project. A learner who claims to be a "hands-on student" may resist a lecture, but later prove capable of engaging deeply in discussion if encouraged. Thus, the problem is not the subject or the method; it is the label that frames the student's perception of what is possible.

Our task as educators is not to force students into a growth box instead of a fixed one, or a kinesthetic box instead of a visual one. Rather, it is to dismantle the boxes altogether. Preferences are real, and moments of discouragement are inevitable, but neither defines a student's capacity. What matters is helping students see that they are more than a label, that persistence matters more than category, and that learning requires flexibility as much as it requires effort.

From Caged to Capable: Restoring a Mindset for Learning

If oversimplified theories have led students to check out, then our job is to replace those labels with something truer and more empowering. Students need to understand that their capacity to learn is not about whether they are "fixed" or "growth," or whether they are a "visual" or "hands-on learner." It is about effort, perseverance, and the belief that their brain itself can change through learning. Therefore, to combat the damage done by the misapplication of Dweck and Gardner, we must bring in what modern research tells us about the brain, and we must shape our classrooms into places where effort is expected and risk-taking feels possible, even safe.

Effort Over Ability

Effort and perseverance are not just helpful for learning; they are the most important aspects of it. Modern cognitive science supports this: Ericsson and Pool's (2016) work on deliberate practice shows that expertise is far less about innate talent than about sustained, purposeful effort over time. Likewise, Robert Sternberg (2005) has argued that engagement and persistence matter more for long-term success than IQ alone.

Throughout my career, I taught the hard stuff: Anatomy and Physiology, Medical Biology, and other advanced sciences. Even students who saw themselves as strong learners often stumbled on the first assessment. When this happened, I used it as a teaching moment. I would pause and point to the Zig Ziglar quote that hung in several places on my classroom walls: *"Do not be disappointed in the results you did not get from the work you did not do."*

Then we would have an honest conversation. I would asked students to reflect on how they had prepared. Had they truly given their best effort? Did they spread their studying over several days, or did they cram the night before? Did they set aside distractions, cell phones, video games, television, or did they allow themselves to be pulled in multiple directions? These questions helped students see that their preparation often fell short of the persistence required for challenging material.

Next, I would ask them to think about something they were really good at—sports, music, dance, gaming—and what it had taken to get there. We would then talk about practice, repetition, and discipline. Sometimes I would even use the example of Tiger Woods, who began swinging a golf club at age three. Natural ability played a role, yes, but perseverance and years of effort were what transformed talent into mastery.

By the end of these conversations, the message was clear: success in science, or in any subject, was not about being born with talent. It was about how hard you were willing to work. I would then challenge students to approach their next assessment with the same mindset they brought to their sport, recital, or tournament, reminding them that the same preparation and commitment that fueled their success elsewhere could also drive their success in the classroom.

The Brain Can Change

Another way to undo the damage of rigid labels is to teach students what neuroscience now makes undeniable: the brain is not static. Learning physically changes the brain, strengthening neural pathways in much the same way exercise strengthens muscles. This idea, known as neuroplasticity, gives students a powerful alternative to the fixed categories they may have internalized.

This was the reasoning behind the Brain Rules Seminar I built into my Anatomy and Physiology course. Anatomy and Physiology is one of the most difficult subjects a high school or undergraduate student can encounter. To succeed, students had to do more than memorize, they had to train their brains to think differently. I wanted them to understand how the brain itself worked so they could tap into it effectively.

John Medina's *Brain Rules* (2008) was our guide. We explored principles such as:

- **Practice boosts brain power.** Just as Tiger Woods developed his swing through practice, our brains need repetition to strengthen learning. This reframed studying as training, not cramming.

- **Stress changes the way we learn.** Too much stress narrows attention, while manageable levels of challenge keep the brain engaged. This helped students understand why waiting until the last minute to prepare often sabotaged their efforts.

- **Sleep is essential.** Sleep consolidates memories. Students often believed staying up late to get more study time would help, but the seminar showed them how lost sleep actually erased the very gains they were working for.

- **We are wired to pay attention to meaning.** The brain filters for relevance. This became a springboard for me to connect physiology concepts to real-world applications (e.g., why heart rate matters in athletics, or how digestion links to nutrition choices) so students would anchor information more deeply.

To reinforce these ideas, I shared research showing that the brain physically changes with learning. Draganski et al. (2004) famously demonstrated that adults who learned to juggle developed measurable increases in gray matter in regions associated with motion and visual processing. Likewise, Maguire et al. (2000) found that London taxi drivers, who must memorize thousands of city streets, had larger hippocampi than average, showing that navigation experience reshaped their brains. Studies like these gave students powerful, visual proof that effort literally rewires the brain.

The seminar opened students' eyes not only to the fact that their brains could grow and change, but also to concrete ways they could partner with that growth. Instead of saying, *"I just can't do this,"* students began asking, *"What can I do to help my brain learn this better?"*

That shift had powerful behavioral consequences. Students were less likely to shut down during difficult tasks and more likely to lean in with persistence. Once they saw their brains as adaptable, they approached challenges as opportunities to strengthen those neural pathways, not as threats to their identity.

Care Creates Courage

If effort is the driver of learning, care is the fuel that makes effort possible. Students take risks when they feel valued, and they persevere when they know someone believes in them. Maya Angelou said it best: *"People will forget what you said, but they will never forget how you made them feel."* When students feel cared for and respected, they are more willing to step into the vulnerable space of learning, even when they think they cannot succeed.

This is where empathy comes in, not as softness that lowers expectations, but as the steady presence that says, *"I believe in you, and I will walk alongside you."* I often use language that communicates partnership rather than command. Instead of saying, *"Here is what **you** are going to do,"* I say, *"Here is what **we** are going to do."* Even small shifts in pronouns matter. They send the message that learning is a shared journey. In fact, throughout this book you may notice how often I write "us," "we," and "our." It is intentional. Learners need to know that educators are not issuing orders from above but joining them in the process.

Word choice also matters when checking for understanding. Asking, *"How many people are ready to move on to the next task?"* feels collaborative and inclusive, while asking, *"How many people need more time?"* can unintentionally spotlight those who are struggling. Similarly, I once had a student teacher who introduced a lesson by saying, with hesitation, *"We are going to **try** to do this."* That phrasing revealed doubt in the students' ability. By contrast, saying, *"We are going to do this"* conveys confidence and communicates belief in students' capacity. Language frames expectation, and expectation shapes behavior.

Care is not only spoken, it is enacted. It shows up in the way we support students without lowering the bar. For example, I provide extra opportunities for success: peer-led review sessions, morning office hours, or late-night email replies to student questions, but I pair that support with the clear expectation that effort is still required. Empathy without accountability becomes permissiveness, and permissiveness undermines both learning and behavior. True care challenges students to rise to their potential while assuring them they will not do it alone.

It also shows up in reliability. Students learn quickly whether a teacher is prepared, consistent, and fair. I hold myself to high standards: arriving on time, being present, grading and giving feedback promptly, and owning when I fall short. I have told students, *"I let you down by not returning your papers when I said that I would, and because of this, I have extended the due date on your next assignment."* Far from diminishing authority, such honesty and flexibility strengthens trust. When students know their teacher is fair and dependable, they mirror that respect in the way they treat the class and one another.

Finally, care creates courage when it balances independence with structure. I value giving students choices in their learning whenever possible, as long as they maintain high personal standards. Independence says, *"I trust you,"* while structure says, *"I expect your best."* Together, they create a climate where students feel both respected and accountable.

In classrooms built on this kind of care, students are not afraid of effort. They know they will be supported, challenged, and treated with dignity. That is when courage takes root; courage to attempt the unfamiliar, to persist when frustrated, and to grow beyond the labels that once held them back.

Research affirms this. Rosenthal and Jacobson's (1968) landmark study on teacher expectations demonstrated that when teachers believed in students' potential, those students actually achieved more, a phenomenon now known as the "Pygmalion effect." When combined with authentic care, high expectations become a powerful motivator for both learning and behavior. Students rise not only because we expect it, but because they feel our belief in them makes it possible.

From effort to brain science to care, the message is the same: students are not defined by labels or locked in cages of identity. They are capable of more than they know when effort is honored, when the brain's ability to grow is made visible, and when care creates the courage to take risks. Therefore, our role as educators is to unlock those cages, remind students that they are not stuck where they started, and walk with them as they discover their own capacity. When we do this, we restore a **Learning Mindset**, and in the process, we strengthen both academic growth and classroom behavior.

Research Spotlight: Nurturing the Pack

Modern research supports what experience in the classroom makes clear: effort, learning, and care are deeply intertwined. Self-determination theory shows that students are most likely to persist when three psychological needs are met: autonomy, competence, and relatedness (Deci & Ryan, 1985; Deci & Ryan, 2000). In simple terms, learners need to feel trusted, capable, and connected.

When these needs are fulfilled, motivation becomes more resilient. Students are less likely to disengage when learning becomes difficult because they experience challenge within the context of safety and belonging.

Research on belonging reinforces this connection. Walton and Cohen (2011) found that even small signals of belonging such as teachers expressing confidence in students' ability to succeed, or gestures that communicate "*you are one of us*" can significantly improve persistence and outcomes, especially for students who fear they do not fit in. Combined with Rosenthal and Jacobson's (1968) findings on teacher expectations, the message is clear: when students believe they are trusted, capable, and part of the classroom pack, they are more likely to lean into challenges instead of backing away from them.

Practical Strategies for Restoring a Learning Mindset

Cultivating a **Learning Mindset** requires steady reinforcement. It is not a one-time lesson but a daily practice that helps students believe in their ability to grow. Here are strategies that keep students engaged, focused, and willing to persist even when learning feels difficult:

1. **Make Effort Visible**
   After assessments, guide students through reflection questions: How did you prepare? How can you prepare differently next time? Pair this with quotes or reminders like Zig Ziglar's, *"Do not be disappointed in the results you did not get from the work you did not do."* Reinforce consistently that results come from persistence, not luck or talent.

2. **Teach the Brain's Ability to Grow**
   Dedicate time early in the year to explain neuroplasticity. For instance, share research, images, or stories that demonstrate how learning strengthens the brain just like exercise strengthens muscles. Refer back to this idea often: This feels hard because your brain is building new pathways. Keep at it—it's proof of growth.

3. **Use Language that Partners, Not Commands**
   Choose pronouns and phrasing that signal shared responsibility. Say *"Here is what* ***we*** *are going to do"* instead of *"Here is what* ***you*** *are*

going to do." When checking for readiness, frame questions in ways that build confidence rather than spotlight struggle.

4. **Balance Empathy with Accountability**
   Offer scaffolds such as review sessions, peer study groups, or extended feedback, but pair them with the clear expectation that effort is nonnegotiable. Care is shown through support, but responsibility for persistence must always remain with the student.

5. **Model Reliability and Fairness**
   Demonstrate what commitment looks like. Be prepared, grade promptly, and acknowledge mistakes openly. When students observe accountability in action, they learn to mirror that same respect and reliability.

6. **Pair Choice with High Standards**
   Provide students with voice in how they learn or demonstrate mastery. Offer options for projects or assignments, while making clear that high effort and quality remain constant expectations. Choice communicates trust, while standards communicate belief in their capability.

Restoring a **Learning Mindset** means helping students navigate struggle rather than avoid it. When these strategies are practiced consistently, they communicate that effort matters, growth is attainable, and care provides stability as students take risks. Over time, those messages shape a classroom climate where students move beyond labels and step into their full potential.

Closing Reflection

Mindset is not about being sorted into categories of "fixed" or "growth," nor is it about being limited to a single learning style. Rather, it is about learning to climb, one step at a time, even when the staircase feels overwhelming. Liberty did not master the stairs because she was naturally gifted. She mastered them because she trusted, tried, and kept moving forward with encouragement. Likewise, students face their own staircases every day. Some hesitate, some retreat, and some move ahead quickly, yet all are capable of climbing when effort is expected, the brain's capacity for growth is revealed, and care steadies them along the way.

As educators, our role is to guide students past the labels that limit them and remind them that capability expands with persistence. When we create classrooms where effort is honored, where science shows the brain can change, and where care makes courage possible, students learn to see themselves differently. From caged to capable, they realize that learning is not defined by who they are now but by who they can become, step by step, with their teacher walking beside them.

Reflection Questions

1. How do you currently talk about effort with your students? Do you emphasize it as the key to growth?
2. In what ways do you explicitly teach students about how the brain learns and changes?
3. How intentional are you with your language? Do your word choices communicate partnership, belief, and care?
4. When students struggle, how do you balance empathy with accountability?

Try This Tomorrow

Growth Language in Action

- Introduce your students to neuroplasticity with a simple explanation, such as, *"Your brain grows stronger every time you practice, just like a muscle."*
- When students encounter a challenging task, remind them, "*This is your brain growing right now.*"
- Notice how this language reframes frustration as evidence of growth, supporting persistence and more regulated behavior.

Chapter 7: Puppy Voice – Enthusiasm is Contagious

Dogs get excited about almost anything if we use the right tone and body language. My experience with this did not come by happenstance. Years ago, I took a weeklong course in dog training on Purdue University's campus. I remember vividly being quite upset when the instructor told us we should not get all excited and make a big deal when we arrive home. I could not understand this at all. After all, isn't part of the joy of sharing your life with a canine that enthusiasm is contagious?

I raised my hand in that large lecture hall and said, *"But I* ***love*** *getting my dogs all excited! Why would I want to stop that?"* The instructor did not miss a beat: *"I bet you do!"* I am pretty sure it was not a compliment, though I chose to take it that way. The advice was well-intended, of course, grounded in avoiding separation anxiety in dogs. Still, I cannot help but make a big deal about everything with my pups. I love that enthusiasm is contagious in the canine world. And believe it or not, it also spreads in the classroom.

Enthusiasm is Infectious

When I walk in the door at home and greet Bella in my high-pitched puppy voice, she does not pause to think about the meaning of my words. Her whole-body wiggles with joy because she feels my excitement. That energy spreads instantly. In classrooms, the same principle applies: students may not consciously analyze every cue we send, but they read our tone, posture, and mood. They catch our enthusiasm!

Research confirms this ripple effect. Frenzel et al., (2024) demonstrated that teacher joy is not a one-way projection but a reciprocal exchange: when teachers expressed enjoyment, students reported higher enjoyment too, which then circled back to the teacher. In other words, enthusiasm feeds a feedback loop, strengthening the emotional climate of the whole classroom.

Lu and colleagues (2025) went even further by measuring physiological responses. They found that students' bodies literally mirrored their teachers' emotions: facial muscles, skin conductance, and heart rhythms shifted in sync with the affect teachers expressed. This shows that contagion is not only psychological but biological; our emotions are quite literally felt in the bodies of those around us.

The same is true with dogs. Siniscalchi and colleagues (2018) showed that dogs process human emotional vocalizations differently depending on tone, even displaying changes in cardiac activity when exposed to happy or angry voices. They also look to human body language and expressions as cues for how to behave in uncertain situations. Bella, for instance, takes her emotional cues from my tone and body language and responds in kind. Likewise, just as dogs absorb our affective cues, students absorb the emotions we project. Enthusiasm spreads, in short, the energy we bring each day can be the spark that shapes how students feel about learning itself.

Project Positivity: Love What You Teach

When dogs tilt their heads and wag their tails, they are responding to the energy we project. Likewise, students quickly pick up on whether we believe our subject is worth their time. If we act bored, they will be bored. If we show fascination, they will be intrigued.

I learned this most vividly while teaching Anatomy and Physiology. Many of my peers shared stories of students dreading dissections, trying to get out of them, or even skipping class altogether. In my classroom, it was the opposite. We counted down the days until dissection. My students knew I loved it, and my enthusiasm made them look forward to it too. If I had expressed dread or offered excuses, I would have sent the message that dissections were unpleasant. But by modeling curiosity and wonder, I reframed the experience before students even formed an opinion.

Research consistently shows that teacher enthusiasm toward subject matter boosts student engagement and achievement. Blazar and Kraft (2016) found that teachers not only impact academic outcomes but also shape students' self-efficacy and happiness in class. Kahveci (2023) reported that students remember teachers' positive attitudes and communication as formative influences on their confidence and motivation. In short: love what you teach, and your students are more likely to love it too.

Bring the Energy – Even Channel a Little Jim Carrey

My husband often jokes that if he tied my hands behind my back, I would no longer be able to speak. He's not far off. I'm a storyteller through and through. When I teach, my arms fly, my face shifts through every expression, and my voice demands attention. Students notice. They cannot help it.

Don't be afraid of that kind of theatrical flair. I've leaned into it in my own teaching: pacing, wide gestures, exaggerated wonder. Sometimes I channel a bit of Jim Carrey energy, not to distract, but to dramatize what's exciting about a concept. When students see you visibly *care*, when your voice rises, your eyes widen, your whole body says *this matters,* they pause. They watch. They lean in.

Dogs remind us of this truth too. They don't just hear our words; they read our posture, our movement, our tone. Bella responds to the whole package. Students do the same.

Activate the Senses to Make Ideas Stick

One of the most powerful ways to teach is by engaging more than words alone, drawing on sight, sound, movement, and emotion at the same time. This approach supports memory. Cognitive science shows that multisensory learning strengthens retention. For instance, current research demonstrates that our sensory modalities interact deeply, so information encoded through multiple senses becomes more strongly integrated and retrievable (Quak, et al., 2015). Further, a recent *Nature* study reinforced this idea, showing that when visual and auditory cues were combined, the brain created cross-modal memory traces that supported stronger recall even when only one sense was later engaged (Okray et al., 2023). For teachers, this means that layering in story, movement, visuals, shifts in tone, and expressive gestures builds more robust scaffolding for memory. In practice, this might look like sketching an idea while telling a story, inviting students to mimic a motion, or letting your face and voice dramatize the weight or wonder of a concept. The more senses you bring into play, the more hooks the memory has to latch on to later.

Research Spotlight: The Power of Visible Enthusiasm

Recent studies show that when teachers project genuine excitement, students don't just notice, they respond. Yan et al., (2023) found that when students perceived their teachers as enthusiastic, their classroom boredom decreased and their engagement increased. The key here is perception: it's not enough for us to feel enthusiastic on the inside. Students must see and hear it in our voice, body language, and delivery.

Burić and colleagues (2020) remind us that enthusiasm is not something we can truly fake. Their research revealed that teacher enthusiasm is linked to intrinsic motivation and well-being. In other words, the more we genuinely love what we teach, the more energy and authenticity we bring to the classroom. Sustaining enthusiasm comes from tending to our own professional joy as much as it does from lesson planning.

Valentín et al., (2022) went one step further by connecting teacher enthusiasm to student outcomes. They found that enthusiastic teaching boosted student interest, which in turn enhanced motivation and achievement. Enthusiasm doesn't just make a lesson more enjoyable in the moment; it can be the pathway that leads students to persist, invest effort, and ultimately succeed.

Together, these studies affirm: enthusiasm is more than a teaching style. It is a catalyst that fills classrooms with the kind of energy where curiosity thrives and the joy of learning becomes contagious.

Practical Strategies for Practicing Puppy-Like Enthusiasm

Harnessing the contagious power of enthusiasm relies on consistent, intentional habits rather than big performances. Here are some ways to make excitement visible and memorable:

1. **Start Strong**
   Begin class with warmth, energy, and an open posture, much like greeting an old friend or a beloved pet. A bright start sets the emotional tone for the entire period.

2. **Celebrate the "Wow" Moments**
   Every subject has them. Name the strange, the beautiful, the astonishing, and let your face and voice reflect genuine amazement. If you light up, your students will too.

3. **Move with Purpose**
   Use your body to emphasize ideas: step forward to stress importance, pause dramatically, or gesture broadly to illustrate scale. Think Jim Carrey-level expression when appropriate; movement reinforces meaning.

4. **Play with Your Voice**
   Inflection, pacing, and volume changes keep students tuned in. Avoid monotone; instead, let your words rise and fall like a story unfolding.

5. **Engage Multiple Senses**
   Pair explanations with visuals, models, stories, or motions. The more senses involved, the more hooks students have for memory.

6. **Share Your Love Out Loud**
   Tell students directly: *"I love teaching this part,"* or *"This is why I became a teacher."* Just as Bella knows my joy from my tone, students need to hear and feel our passion.

Closing Reflection

We recently adopted a retired racing Greyhound named Bear, and from the very first day, he bonded with me instantly. So much so that whenever I left the house, he would pee on the floor by the very door I had gone out of if he was left alone with my husband. Something had to give. My husband is a man's man with a deep, booming voice, but I knew what Bear needed. He needed the puppy voice. When my husband finally asked, at his wits' end, *"What can I do?"* I said, *"You're not going to like it! But you need to use the puppy voice."* With an eye roll, he agreed to try. Within 48 hours, Bear was wagging his tail with delight when my husband walked in and no longer peeing on the floor. The puppy voice mattered. It always does.

In the classroom, the same principle holds true. Our enthusiasm, our warmth, our tone, those small choices in how we present ourselves, can change the way students respond to us and to learning. Just like Bear, students may not analyze every word, but they absolutely feel the energy behind them. And when we choose to project joy, curiosity, and care, our students, like Bear, begin to meet us at the door of learning with tails wagging.

Reflection Questions

1. Think of a teacher you once had who showed obvious enthusiasm for their subject. How did it affect your experience in that class?
2. How do your students know that you enjoy what you teach? What cues, verbal or nonverbal, make it visible to them?
3. When do you feel your enthusiasm wane in the classroom? What strategies help you re-energize in those moments?
4. How might you make your own love of the subject more visible?

Try This Tomorrow

Lead With Joy

- Choose one small part of your lesson to introduce with visible enthusiasm.
- Smile, lift your voice, and lean in with your whole body as you begin.
- Notice how students respond when you model genuine joy for learning.

Chapter 8: Unleashing Motivation – Inspiring the Drive Within

One of the first things a dog trainer will tell us is to figure out what motivates the dog we want to train. Some dogs are treat motivated. Others light up at praise or affection. Some will do almost anything for their favorite toy. Whatever it is, that motivation becomes the key to teaching them, because when they *want* to work for us, their learning is limitless.

With humans, motivation is more complex. Students need more than praise and rewards. They are driven by factors such as belonging, relevance, meaningful choices, appropriate challenge, recognition of their progress, moments of novelty, and a sense of purpose. When these needs are met, something powerful begins to take hold: students actually *want* to work hard. The question, then, becomes this: how can we design a learning environment that truly unleashes motivation?

Belonging: The Leash that Connects Us

In Chapter 5, we focused on building the foundation by learning our students' stories, earning their trust, fostering peer-relations, and creating the emotional safety that allows authentic relationships to grow. Once that sense of belonging is established, something remarkable happens: it drives motivation.

Belonging changes how students see themselves as learners. It turns *the* classroom into *our* classroom. When students feel part of something bigger than themselves, their motivation shifts. They stop performing for approval and begin participating for connection. They want to do well not only for their own sake, but because they care about the shared success of the group.

I saw this play out most clearly during group projects. Students would begin talking excitedly about how they could continue working together outside of class. They planned meetups at local coffee shops, came to my classroom during study hall, and coordinated after school schedules so one student could take the project home and another could pick it up the next day. They even stopped by to share their progress with me because they were proud of what they had created together and wanted me to be part of that success.

Their motivation was rooted in relationships, both with one another and with me, and that sense of belonging fueled their effort.

That same motivation surfaced when students prepared for assessments. Nearly every year, I learned that most students had exchanged phone numbers and were helping one another study for upcoming tests. They shared notes, quizzed each other, and clarified misunderstandings. Inspired by this, I added a peer help section to my online learning management system. Students embraced it immediately. The message was clear: we are in this together. Their motivation increased because their success was no longer an individual pursuit, but a shared responsibility.

These shifts also appeared in quieter moments. A student double checking their work because they did not want to let a lab partner down. A peer offering encouragement when someone was struggling. This mirrors what we see in a well bonded dog who works not just for treats, but because the relationship itself matters. In this way, belonging transforms motivation from external to internal, and from compliance to commitment.

Belonging is the motivation. Students naturally integrate **Three Before Me** and turn to one another before turning to the teacher. They show up prepared, persist through challenge, and celebrate progress together. They are not working only for a grade. They are working because their effort matters to others. When students feel valued and connected, they stay engaged even when the work becomes demanding. Belonging anchors effort in purpose and connection, holding the group together and creating a classroom environment where students genuinely *want* to work hard.

Relevance: Make it Matter

Relevance is the bridge that links effort to meaning in the moment. When the purpose of learning feels distant or disconnected from a student's world, engagement weakens. Relevance answers the silent question students carry into every lesson: *Why does this matter?* When we connect new learning to something they care about, motivation deepens and persistence grows. Although curriculum maps and pacing guides can make it seem as if we do not have time for relevance, taking a moment to show students why something matters often saves time later. When students understand the purpose behind a lesson, they lean in, form stronger connections, and retain more, which reduces the need for reteaching.

In science courses, this might mean connecting an anatomy lesson to patient care, or exploring how cellular respiration relates to athletic performance. In English, it might involve analyzing persuasive techniques used in social media or current events. Whatever the subject, relevance transforms abstract ideas into experiences that feel alive.

Relevance also grows when we invite students to share their own connections. When they link content to personal interests or lived experiences, they take ownership. They begin to explore, inquire, and make sense of the world on their own terms. I have watched entire classes light up when a student connects a concept to athletics, clinical practice, or something they noticed in their daily life. These moments remind everyone that learning is personal long before it is academic.

Research supports what teachers see every day. When students find personal meaning in content, the brain becomes more receptive to learning. Explaining ideas, discussing them, applying them, and generating examples activates multiple regions of the brain and strengthens neural pathways that support long-term retention (GSI Teaching and Resource Center, 2023). Self-determination theory reinforces this as well. When relevance enhances a sense of purpose and personal value, motivation and engagement rise naturally (Ryan and Deci, 2017).

Relevance shows students that what we teach extends beyond the classroom. Knowledge becomes practical, transferable, and connected to everyday life. When learning feels purposeful and personal, motivation follows, and the desire to participate becomes intrinsic rather than enforced.

Choice and Voice: Students' Turn to Lead

Motivation deepens further when students feel that their voices matter. When they have some control over how they learn and how they show what they know, the learning becomes even more personal. Choice does not mean handing over all control; it means inviting students into the process and trusting them to share ownership of their learning.

When we give students the chance to make meaningful choices, something changes in the energy of the room. They begin to view themselves as partners in learning rather than passengers. Even small decisions, such as choosing a topic for a project, selecting how to present their understanding, or determining how to organize their work, can turn compliance into commitment.

One of my favorite examples of this came from my dual credit Biology class. As a culminating project, small groups of students were challenged to teach their own lesson. I provided a basic structure that included a hook, content delivery, guided practice, and a short formative assessment. From there, everything was up to them. They selected the topic, designed the visuals, created the activities, and even developed their own quiz questions. The results were incredible. Each group brought its own creativity, humor, and insight to the task, and the classroom buzzed with excitement. It was often referenced as their favorite project of the year, solely because it belonged to them. When students experience this level of ownership, their motivation naturally deepens. Our role shifts from directing every move to guiding and supporting their exploration.

Choice and voice also grow when we take time to listen. Asking students what helps them learn, what confuses them, or what they wish we would do differently can reveal what truly motivates them. When we act on their feedback, we show that their voices shape the classroom. That trust builds confidence and encourages students to take even greater initiative.

When students feel both trusted and heard, their confidence expands. They approach learning with curiosity rather than fear. Choice and voice give learners a sense of agency, transforming the classroom from a place where learning is done *to* them into a space where learning is done *with* them.

Challenge: Stretch Without Snapping

Every learner needs the right balance between comfort and challenge. If the work is too easy, motivation fades. If it feels impossible, frustration takes over. The goal is to find that middle ground where students feel stretched just enough to grow, but still supported enough to believe they can succeed.

Confidence grows through experiences of success, even in small steps. Those moments of success give students courage to take greater risks, and those risks are where meaningful learning happens. Our role is to create conditions where challenge feels attainable and progress is visible, helping students see that effort and reflection, not innate ability, are what move them forward.

One powerful way to maintain that balance is to teach students to self-assess. McMillan and Hearn (2008) define self-assessment as a process in which students monitor and evaluate the quality of their thinking and behavior while learning and identify strategies to improve understanding and skills. When students engage in this ongoing cycle of self-monitoring, self-evaluation, and correction, they develop the internal tools that drive motivation. They begin to take responsibility for their own learning rather than waiting for us to judge it.

I used this approach during the lesson teaching project in my dual credit Biology class by embedding checkpoints throughout their process. At each checkpoint, students paused to reflect on what was working, what needed clarification, and what adjustments they could make before continuing. Those pauses became moments of metacognition, when students actively thought about their own thinking and learning. Through that reflection, students identified what could be refined and improved as they moved forward. The checkpoints transformed challenge into progress.

Research supports what I saw in practice. When students are taught how to self-assess, they tend to persist longer, show greater confidence, and take more ownership of their work. They also learn to attribute success to effort and strategy rather than luck or innate ability, which strengthens motivation and self-efficacy (McMillan & Hearn, 2008).

We can reinforce this mindset by designing lessons that include natural pauses for reflection and correction. Clear learning goals, rubrics, and exemplars that show levels of proficiency help students see what growth looks like in concrete terms. I saw the power of exemplars play out year after year. In my Anatomy and Physiology class, students created life size models of body systems. I saved exceptional projects from previous years and shared them with incoming classes as a vision for what was possible. Each year, the work improved in accuracy, detail, and creativity. Eventually, the projects filled the hallways, and colleagues noticed the steady rise in quality. Students were not intimidated by the examples. They were motivated by them.

The same principle applied to written work. In my dual credit Biology class, students wrote paragraphs explaining cellular respiration. I saved strong examples from previous years and shared them aloud with new students. I did not allow copying or photographing. Instead, students listened for clarity, precision, and depth. Exemplars made expectations visible without pressure. They raised the bar while still meeting students where they were.

When students understand that challenge is an opportunity for growth rather than a judgment of worth, they rise to meet it. They persist, adjust, and trust their ability to improve because the path forward feels clear and attainable. In that balance between support and struggle, motivation takes root, and students learn how to stretch without snapping.

Recognition: Paws to Celebrate

Every task feels lighter when we pause to celebrate how far we've come, even learning. Recognition fuels motivation when it focuses on effort, persistence, and growth. Students who feel that their progress is seen and valued are more likely to keep moving forward, even when the work becomes difficult.

Meaningful recognition is not about gold stars or empty praise. It is about helping students see themselves as capable learners. When we point out the strategies they used, the determination they showed, or the improvement they made, we shift their attention from performance to process. This reinforces the belief that success comes from effort, reflection, and perseverance rather than from natural ability.

I learned this lesson early in my teaching career when a student who had struggled for weeks finally mastered a difficult concept. When I told her exactly what I had noticed, her persistence, her willingness to ask questions, and her thoughtful approach, her expression said everything. She did not just feel proud of the result; she felt proud of the *work* that led her there. That kind of recognition builds lasting motivation because it celebrates who the student is becoming, not just what the student produces.

Recognition also builds community. When we take time to celebrate collective achievements, students feel connected to something larger than themselves. In my classes, I often highlight moments of growth that happen quietly: the student who took the lead in helping a peer, the group that worked through confusion together, or the class that improved its lab results through collaboration. When we honor those moments, we reinforce the idea that learning is shared and that every contribution matters.

This kind of celebration does not have to be elaborate. Sometimes it is a simple note in the margin of a paper, a few words at the end of class, or a public acknowledgment of effort. What matters is authenticity. Students know when praise is sincere, and they respond to it by setting higher goals and believing in their capacity to reach them.

When recognition focuses on mastery rather than comparison, it cultivates what researchers call a mastery orientation (Ames, 1992; Dweck, 1986). Through a mastery-oriented lens, students view learning as a journey of improvement rather than a contest of ability. They persist longer, recover more quickly from setbacks, and take greater pride in growth than in grades. This mindset has the power to transform the atmosphere of the classroom where success is something shared, and each step forward, no matter how small, feels worth celebrating.

Novelty: Keep the Tail Wagging

Motivation thrives on curiosity. When students feel a sense of surprise or discovery, learning comes alive. Novelty captures attention and invites engagement because it interrupts the ordinary. It offers a small mystery or twist that pulls students forward and reminds them that learning can still surprise them.

One of my favorite ways to introduce mystery is through case studies that spark inquiry. In my dual credit Biology class, I used a mysterious case study based on the 1982 Tylenol poisonings, when several people in the Chicago area died after ingesting Tylenol capsules laced with potassium cyanide (Dreisbach & Robertson, 1987). Students were able to determine relatively quickly that the Tylenol was responsible for the deaths, but the real challenge came in understanding *how* cyanide killed the victims. To do that, they had to explore the details of cellular respiration and understand how cyanide binds to cytochrome c oxidase, preventing cells from using oxygen and halting aerobic metabolism (Schaffer et al., 2025). This was one of the most difficult case studies I incorporated, but the curiosity it generated made it one of the most engaging. Students were determined to uncover the answer, and that drive kept them focused far beyond the surface level.

Novelty can also come from giving students freedom in how they show what they know. In my Anatomy and Physiology class, students created music videos to demonstrate anatomical body movements such as plantar flexion, dorsiflexion, and rotation. The results were creative, funny, and impressively accurate. Because the format was their choice, they took ownership of the work and took pride in the outcome. What might have been a simple vocabulary task became an experience of shared laughter and genuine learning.

At its best, novelty reminds students that learning is dynamic and alive. It helps them see that curiosity is not something to outgrow, but something to cultivate. When they approach learning with wonder, motivation follows naturally. The tail keeps wagging because the mind is still exploring.

Purpose: Why it Matters Beyond a Grade

Students are often most motivated when they believe their work has meaning beyond the classroom. Purpose gives direction to effort. It reminds students that what they are learning connects to something larger, whether that is a personal goal, a career path, or the desire to make a difference. When students understand the purpose behind what they are doing, motivation begins to rise from within rather than from external rewards.

Purpose can take many forms. For some students, it is tied to their future careers. For others, it comes from realizing that what they learn can make a difference in someone else's life. In my Anatomy and Physiology classes, purpose often emerged when students made connections between content and patient care. When they recognized that mastering a concept could someday help them save a life or ease someone's pain, the motivation became deeply personal. They were no longer studying for a grade; they were preparing for the responsibility that comes with their chosen profession.

Purpose also grows when students see it modeled. During the six years I spent earning my master's and doctoral degrees while teaching full time, my students shared in that journey. I often talked about the late nights, the courses that challenged me, and the strategies I used to push through. When I was taking a particularly demanding class on the immune system, I created several large concept maps, visual diagrams that organize and connect ideas, just to keep all the information straight. Those maps became my lifeline, and I brought them to class to show my students how I was using them to learn. They saw my tenacity in real time. I did not just talk about perseverance; I practiced it. Over time, they began to share that I was both the hardest-working teacher and the hardest-working student they had ever met. More importantly, it made them think about their own goals and the paths they would take to reach them.

As teachers, we can nurture this same sense of purpose by helping students see themselves as contributors. When they create resources for future classes, explain ideas to peers, or design tools others can use, they recognize the value of their growing expertise. Learning takes on meaning because it serves something beyond the grade.

Purpose does not remove challenge, but it reshapes it. Obstacles feel worthwhile when the work aligns with what students hope to become. Even when they stumble, learners who understand their purpose are more likely to get back up and try again.

Purpose anchors motivation. It reminds students that learning extends beyond points earned to the influence their knowledge can have on the world.

The Power of Influence

As teachers, we hold tremendous power. With a single word, expression, or decision, we can lift a student's confidence or unintentionally erode it. The stronger the bond, the greater the influence.

There are times when our good intentions can lead us astray. One well-known example of this came from the Pizza Hut "Book It" program, which rewarded students with free pizza for reading a certain number of books (Kohn, 2018). At first, participation skyrocketed. Even reluctant readers joined in. But over time, something subtle happened. The students who once read for joy began choosing shorter, easier books to earn more coupons. When the program ended, many of those same students stopped reading altogether. The external reward had replaced their internal reason to read. Motivation that once came from curiosity and satisfaction was replaced by the promise of pizza, and when the reward disappeared, so did the motivation.

The same lesson applies to our classrooms. Rewards and incentives can have a place, but they must never replace purpose or curiosity. Students should not work for the sticker, the **Thank You Slip**, or the extra credit. They should work because the learning feels meaningful, and because we have helped them see that meaning. Our influence must build motivation, not borrow it.

There is another kind of influence that requires equal care. It happens not through what we give, but through how deeply our students trust us. I once had a student who consistently performed at a very high level. On one exam, she scored much lower than usual. After class, she told me that she was feeling upset because she was afraid of what I would think of her. She worried that one score would change my opinion of her. I was shocked by the emotion in her voice. To me, she was bright, capable, and confident, but she revealed how vulnerable even the strongest students can feel.

That moment stayed with me. It reminded me that students carry our words, our tone, and even our silence with them. They measure themselves through our reactions far more than we realize. In that moment, I knew what mattered most was to reassure her. I told her that one test score could never change how much I believed in her, and that my respect for her effort would never depend on a number.

Our influence as teachers can ignite motivation or quietly extinguish it. The difference often lies in intention and awareness. Whether we are offering encouragement, feedback, or recognition, we must do so with compassion and perspective. Influence, when guided by empathy, becomes a powerful force for growth. When it is unexamined, it can unintentionally create fear or dependence.

The power of influence calls us to be mindful of how we motivate. It reminds us that our words and choices matter long after the lesson ends. When we use that power to affirm worth, model perseverance, and nurture purpose, our students carry that belief into every challenge they face. That is the kind of motivation that lasts.

Research Spotlight: The Science of Motivation

As discussed earlier, motivation flourishes when students experience belonging, autonomy, and competence. Self-determination theory provides the framework, but it is classroom design that brings these needs to life (Ryan & Deci, 2017).

Belonging grows when relationships are intentionally cultivated and classroom community is made visible through shared norms, such as emoji name plates or routines like **Three Before Me**, that signal to students that they are seen, supported, and part of the learning community. Autonomy develops when students are offered meaningful choices and a sense of voice in their learning. Competence strengthens when learners experience success at appropriately challenging tasks and receive timely, actionable feedback.

Research consistently confirms that students who perceive their teachers as autonomy supportive, those who provide meaningful choices, encourage self-direction, and foster connection, demonstrate higher engagement, deeper learning, and stronger persistence across disciplines (Ryan & Deci, 2017). Motivation, then, is not driven primarily by grades or external rewards. It emerges when learning environments help students feel capable, connected, and in control of their growth.

When instruction is designed with these needs in mind, motivation rises from within, sustained by purpose, relevance, and genuine engagement.

Practical Strategies for Keeping the Drive Alive

Motivation, thus, comes from the ongoing pattern of belonging, relevance, voice, challenge, recognition, novelty, and purpose. Each of these must be revisited, adjusted, and nurtured as our students grow. The following practices are simple ways to keep motivation steady and sustainable throughout the year.

1. **Build in Regular Reflection**
   Give students consistent space to reflect on their progress. Quick check-ins, 3x5 reflections, or "what I learned today" cards help them internalize self-assessment and recognize growth.

2. **Offer Choices that Matter**
   Choice does not have to mean unlimited options. Even a small decision such as topic selection, order of completion, or format of demonstration, gives students a sense of control that builds engagement.
3. **Connect Content to Life**
   Regularly pause to explain *why* something matters. Ask, *"Where might this show up in your future career or daily life?"* and let students discover the connection themselves.
4. **Recognize Effort Authentically**
   Point out persistence, creativity, and problem-solving more often than correct answers. Recognition that focuses on the process strengthens motivation far more than extrinsic rewards ever could.
5. **Keep Curiosity Alive**
   Add one small moment of novelty or surprise each week. A "mystery of the day," an unexpected demonstration, or a puzzling question keeps curiosity engaged and learning fresh.
6. **Model Your Own Motivation**
   Share your goals, challenges, and learning strategies with your students. Let them see that perseverance and purpose are not lessons you teach; they are values you live by.

Closing Reflection

Motivation is something we cultivate through intentional practices. Much like a young dog that grows confident through steady encouragement, students thrive when they feel safe, valued, and capable of meeting new challenges. When belonging is strong, when learning feels meaningful, and when students are given room to make choices and take ownership, motivation is unleashed and rises from within.

Reflection Questions

1. Which of the motivational drivers (belonging, relevance, voice, challenge, recognition, novelty, or purpose) feels most natural for you to cultivate? Which requires more intentional effort?
2. Think of a time when a student surprised you with their motivation. What conditions allowed that to happen?

3. How can you ensure that your recognition practices emphasize effort and growth rather than innate ability or extrinsic rewards?
4. How might you model your own perseverance or sense of purpose for students this semester?

Try This Tomorrow

Motivation Moments

- Set aside five minutes at the end of class for students to reflect on motivation.
- Ask students to write down one moment when they felt curious, capable, or proud during the lesson.
- Select a few responses to read aloud at the start of the next class.
- Use this routine to reinforce that motivation is intentionally built, nurtured, and celebrated over time.

Part 3: Leader of the Pack

Classroom management is as much about us as it is about the students. It is our preparation, our consistency, and our presence. When things are not going well, I have learned to start with the mirror. Did I follow my own protocols? Did I greet students warmly and make them feel valued before I launched into the lesson? Did I have everyone's attention before giving directions? Was my tone steady, my pacing clear, my task engaging, my expectations explicit? If the answer to any of these is no, then I know where to begin.

There's no doubt that classroom management begins, and ends, with our leadership. The best leaders, whether of dogs or students, set clear expectations, anticipate needs, and create environments where others can thrive. In the dog-training world, there is a saying: *a tired dog is a good dog.* The idea isn't about exhaustion but about fulfillment. A dog who has been given a job, stimulation, and purpose is calmer and more content. The same is true for our students. When learners are mentally engaged and challenged at the right level, their energy has direction and focus. Well-designed lessons don't drain students; they satisfy them.

If Part 1 laid out the *rules* of the game and Part 2 explored the *heart* of it, then this part is about how to *coach* the game, how to guide and inspire those we lead. It is about the choices and mindsets that allow a classroom to buzz with focus and joy. Success, of course, does not mean perfection; it means learning to navigate the ebb and flow of real classroom life. Some days, everything clicks, students are engaged, lessons flow, and you can feel the energy of learning. Other days remind us that even the best plans need adjustment. Leadership means knowing how to steer the pack when the trail gets bumpy, to stay consistent, compassionate, and calm while finding a new way forward.

These final chapters wrap up what it means to lead with balance, purpose, and humanity:

- **A Tired Dog is a Good Dog – Setting Students up for Success**
- **Correction – The Least Invasive Approach**
- **Teaching Old Dogs New Tricks – The Five R's of Classroom Renewal**
- **Tail-Wagging Takeaways – Pack Leader Wrap-Ups**

Classroom management is the true art of teaching. It blends structure, care, and leadership into a rhythm that gives students an emotionally safe environment where they can take risks, engage their minds, and, hopefully, become lifelong lovers of learning.

Chapter 9: A Tired Dog is a Good Dog – Setting Students up for Success

Bear, our retired racing Greyhound, has been teaching us a lot about energy lately. At six years old, he is younger and far more energetic than Bella, our steady Great Dane. The concept of *a tired dog is a good dog* couldn't be more relevant as I write this chapter. It is fall, and the weekend was full of dangerous thunderstorms, high winds, and steady rain. Our usual two walks and a daily ball throw was replaced with restless pacing and whining. By Sunday night, Bear was bouncing off the walls, discontent and fidgety, and far from the calm, chill dude we know.

Finally, laughing at ourselves as we zipped ponchos and tugged on the dogs' raincoats, we braved the storm for a brisk, cool walk. The change was immediate. Our sweet, relaxed boy was back. A tired dog, we realized once again, is indeed a good dog.

While being tired is good for dog behavior, things are a bit different when it comes to students. They do not learn well when they are worn out or depleted. Instead, students find their stride through purposeful and thought-provoking activity. When they are invited to participate, think, talk, create, and engage with ideas, their energy settles into mental focus. This shift forms the heart of active instruction, a practice that channels student energy into curiosity and productive effort.

Active learning is how humans learn best, yet it only thrives when the classroom environment is steady and predictable. Everything we built in earlier chapters, from routines to relationships, was designed to support this moment. When those pieces are in place, active instruction can bloom, and students can give their best thinking without confusion, hesitation, or fear.

Active instruction is the educational equivalent of a well-planned training session. It replaces long stretches of passive listening with short, intentional bursts of input, practice, movement, and discussion. The teacher is a facilitator who designs experiences, sets the pace, and guides the energy of the room toward meaningful work. Through active instruction strategies, we engage students mentally and set them up for success.

Fulfillment, Not Fatigue

The goal of teaching is not to wear students out but to fill them up with curiosity, creativity, and connection. A disengaged mind looks for distraction, but an engaged mind settles into the work. True engagement grows out of meaningful work. When students are challenged, supported, and invited to think deeply, they leave class feeling the satisfying kind of tired that comes from purpose.

Students do not need more time sitting and listening; they need time thinking, creating, and collaborating. When lessons balance cognitive challenge with opportunities for action, students channel their energy into productive focus. They associate learning with fulfillment rather than frustration. A student who has spent the class building, analyzing, or explaining feels a quiet pride, not exhaustion, but accomplishment.

Brain-based research supports what experienced teachers know instinctively: learning that engages multiple senses and actions strengthens understanding and retention. When students move, discuss, and create, their brains form stronger connections between ideas, increasing comprehension and recall (GSI Teaching & Resource Center, 2023). In other words, students learn best when they are active participants, not passive recipients.

Active instruction requires presence and pacing. Teachers set the tempo, alternating between short bursts of focused input and moments for students to process, apply, or reflect. This approach keeps energy steady and attention sustained. The timer we introduced at the start of the year was never just about structure. It was an early signal that learning would move with intention and purpose. Think intervals, not marathons. Think purpose, not busyness. When instructional flow aligns with the way students learn, the classroom buzzes with focus and calm, a space where minds are busy and spirits are at ease.

When students are fully engaged, their energy becomes focused rather than scattered. The question then becomes: How can we create an environment that supports this kind of focus? The good news is that we set the foundation early through consistent routines, clear procedures, and meaningful relationships. Classrooms flourish when expectations are steady and students feel known and supported. In that kind of environment, they settle into their work because the room communicates safety and purpose. With this groundwork in place, we can design learning that moves, challenges, and inspires. We shape the pace, model the processes, and provide steady guidance. As we do, the classroom flourishes and reflects the behaviors we hope to see. In an active and well supported space, students respond with attention, curiosity, and a willingness to try because the expectations around them invite those habits.

Age Plus Two, Chunking, and Scaffolding

Attention is not infinite; it ebbs and flows like a muscle that must be rested to work at its best. One simple guide, often called the **Age Plus Two** rule, suggests that students can focus for approximately their age plus two minutes before attention begins to wane. A sixteen-year-old, then, can listen intently for about eighteen minutes before the brain needs to pause, shift, or move. While no rule fits every learner, it is a helpful reminder that sustained focus requires intentional design.

The solution is not to demand longer stretches of concentration but to structure lessons that respect natural spans of attention. Plan short, purposeful bursts of input followed by moments for students to process, apply, or discuss. A brief pair-share, a quick reflection on a whiteboard, or a chance to stand and compare answers can reset energy and prepare the brain for the next burst of learning.

Chunking and scaffolding extend this idea beyond timing to the way we organize information. Cognitive psychology shows that the brain retains and retrieves material more efficiently when it is presented in small, connected pieces rather than in large, unbroken blocks. Breaking complex concepts into smaller, sequential steps, each building on the last, helps students experience success early and maintain confidence as the work becomes more demanding.

Scaffolding is the art of balance: giving enough support to make success possible, then gradually removing that support as independence grows. When students see each piece link smoothly to the next, they recognize that learning is a process rather than a test of instant mastery. They begin to trust that the challenge ahead is achievable because it builds on what they already know.

Short, intentional intervals and carefully layered instruction protect attention, prevent frustration, and keep learners moving forward. In a well-paced classroom, instead of feeling rushed or restless; students feel guided.

Student Leaders and Peer Teaching

Dogs often learn best from watching another dog complete a task successfully. The same social dynamic exists in the classroom. When students teach one another, understanding deepens on both sides, the one explaining consolidates learning, and the one listening receives it in a language closer to their own.

Assigning student leaders transforms the classroom into a collaborative learning community. Begin by designating a leader in each small group, and only give those students the next set of directions. They return to their groups to share the task, model the first step, and guide the team's work. This structure immediately changes the listening dynamic: students pay closer attention when they know they will soon explain the task to others.

Rotating leadership ensures that every student practices both giving and receiving guidance. Over time, these roles build communication, confidence, and accountability. Leadership shifts from control to service, helping peers move forward together.

Peer teaching can take many forms: a quick "teach-back" at the end of a mini-lesson, a peer-led review station, or a "leader huddle" where group representatives meet with the teacher for one minute of coaching before returning to brief their teams. Each variation encourages autonomy and peer connection, two factors closely linked to motivation and retention (Ryan & Deci, 2017).

When students become resources for one another, the teacher's voice no longer needs to fill every moment. The room purrs with shared ownership. The focus shifts from *"What does the teacher want?"* to *"What do we need to understand together?"* That shift transforms classroom management from supervision to partnership.

Space Matters: Seating and Grouping

The design of a classroom silently communicates its expectations. Before a single word is spoken, the arrangement of desks, the openness of space, and the visibility of materials send messages about how learning will unfold. Rows signal listening. Circles invite dialogue. Clusters suggest collaboration. In this way, physical space serves as a nonverbal cue for behavior and engagement.

Intentional seating and grouping are essential tools for success. When students can easily see one another, conversation becomes natural. When materials are within reach, transitions are smoother. Therefore, we must arrange the room for the work we want to see. If the task is collaborative, group students so they face one another and can share materials comfortably. If we need quick shifts from whole-class focus to small-group discussion, we, then, keep pathways open and supplies organized at the edges of the room. We can also use stable base groups for long-term trust building, and flexible "quick turn" groups for variety and movement.

Group dynamics deserve the same care as physical arrangement. Rotate roles within groups, such as leader, materials manager, researcher, and timekeeper, so that responsibility is shared and every student's voice has value. Post success criteria or checklists where students can see them, ensuring they know what progress looks like without relying on constant teacher direction.

A thoughtfully organized space reduces behavioral challenges before they begin. When movement, visibility, and expectations are built into the environment, students know how to participate and where to direct their attention. The classroom feels purposeful and alive, not crowded or chaotic.

Hands On, Minds On: Concrete to Abstract

Students learn best when they can work with a concrete idea before moving to an abstract one. Hands on learning transforms concepts into experiences, giving students the opportunity to build understanding rather than memorize definitions. When they manipulate, observe, or create something tangible, they connect theory to practice and deepen comprehension. In short, learning moves from passive reception to active construction, and meaning becomes something students build for themselves rather than something delivered to them.

As teachers, we can help students enter learning through the concrete. For example, when we give them something to hold, shape, or move that mirrors the concept, we offer an accessible starting point. In anatomy, this might be building a model of a sarcomere from clay or arranging colored beads to represent the base pairs of DNA. In chemistry, magnets can serve as ionic bonds showing attraction between oppositely charged ions, while interlocking pieces such as paper clips or Lego bricks can illustrate covalent bonds where electrons are shared. Once students have interacted with the physical representation, we can then invite them to label, explain, and reflect on how structure supports function.

When students teach what they have created, abstract understanding becomes anchored in visible evidence. For instance, asking students to record short videos explaining their model's function turns a hands-on activity into a clear demonstration of comprehension. In fact, these activities engage multiple regions of the brain, visual, motor, and linguistic, which strengthens neural connections and deepens retention (GSI Teaching and Resource Center, 2023).

Concept mapping also offers a powerful bridge from concrete to abstract. In particular, when we provide a partial map frame and a list of terms and phrases, students can physically arrange and connect ideas. Another approach, one that makes student thinking visible, is for students to collaboratively draw the map directly on their desks with chalk markers. As students link terms and justify their relationships aloud, we can observe understanding in real time.

Hands on learning does more than make lessons enjoyable; it gives students the experience of discovery. They are not told how systems connect; they uncover it. And as they move from building to explaining to applying, the transition from concrete to abstract unfolds naturally. Students remember what they make, manipulate, and teach, because those experiences become theirs.

Interactive Mini Lectures

Even the most active classrooms sometimes need direct instruction. The goal is to keep those moments brief, purposeful, and engaging. A mini lecture, when used well, shifts from simple information delivery to a spark for curiosity and a guide toward student discovery.

The human brain craves novelty and interaction. Research in cognitive science shows that attention fades when learners passively receive information but revives when they are asked to think, respond, or move (GSI Teaching and Resource Center, 2023). In any event, our aim is to make lecture moments interactive so they feel like experiences rather than monologues.

To begin, we can anchor each lecture with a question, problem, or visual that invites students to wonder. Then, we pause often and let them write, sketch, or talk through their thinking. Dry erase boards work well for quick responses, and digital polls offer instant feedback. After a few minutes of input, we can add small opportunities for movement: stand to share an idea, compare notes with someone new, or rotate to another table for discussion. Even simple shifts in position reawaken attention and help new learning stick.

Interactive lectures honor our expertise while presenting it in digestible bursts. A five-minute explanation, a short demonstration, and a few minutes of peer processing often support deeper understanding than a lengthy talk. To conclude each segment, we can offer a brief synthesis question such as *"What did we just uncover?"* or *"How does this connect to what we learned yesterday?"* so students can name and claim their learning.

When students are active participants in instruction, they are not merely listening; they are rehearsing understanding in real time. The classroom energy changes from compliance to curiosity, from stillness to focus. The lecture becomes not a break from learning, but a bridge to it.

Movement and Tempo

Movement can be a powerful tool for focus. Attention is a physical process as well as a mental one. When students sit too long, attention wanes and energy turns inward, often surfacing as off task behavior. However, purposeful movement reactivates attention and channels that energy toward learning.

Research supports what teachers observe every day: physical activity increases blood flow to the brain, which enhances alertness and cognitive performance (Ratey, 2008). Even brief shifts such as standing to talk, walking to compare ideas, or changing seats can reset focus. The key is to use movement strategically so each transition supports a learning goal.

For example, standing conversations work well for short discussions. We can ask students to find someone they have not worked with, share one idea, and listen to one in return. Keeping it brief, three minutes or less, allows everyone to return ready to summarize key takeaways. Gallery walks, where students move around the room to view and respond to posted work, also provide meaningful movement as students circulate to observe work in progress and offer feedback. Lab stations, where students rotate through different tasks or activities, add another layer of motion, allowing students to rotate through tasks and apply content in multiple contexts.

Tempo matters as much as movement. The classroom's pacing communicates its expectations and helps shape the learning experience. A predictable tempo reduces anxiety and supports flow. Students should sense a pattern: input, process, move, reflect. This sequence keeps them grounded and engaged. Visible timers, clear transitions, and consistent cues help students understand where they are in the learning process.

When movement is purposeful and pacing is steady, the classroom feels alive without becoming chaotic. My former principal used to call this *controlled chaos*. It was exactly what he hoped to see during observations, an environment that might appear hectic at first glance but reveals students actively engaging with the material the moment you look closer. Students shift their attention because they are curious, not because they are restless. The goal is sustained engagement, a balance between motion and meaning that keeps energy flowing and minds settled into the work.

Visible Thinking

Learning deepens when students can see their own thought process unfold. When ideas stay invisible, it is difficult for both students and teachers to know what is truly understood. Making thinking visible turns learning into something observable, sharable, and actionable.

One of the simplest ways to make thinking visible is through whiteboards or chalk markers. When every student writes, draws, or models an answer at the same time, the room represents a snapshot of collective reasoning. This approach normalizes participation because every hand is moving and every voice has something to contribute. Collecting a few examples for quick discussion allows you to highlight strong reasoning and gently address misconceptions before they take root.

In addition, technology can support this process. Tools such as Pear Deck, Kahoot, or digital polls provide real time insight into understanding. Yet visible thinking does not depend on devices. Quick writes, pair-shares, exit slips, and one-minute reflections serve the same purpose. They make thought tangible. When students articulate what they know and what they are still wondering, they actively monitor their own learning, a skill central to growth and independence.

Visible thinking also builds community. As students notice that everyone is thinking, questioning, and revising, learning is viewed as a shared journey rather than a solitary task. Mistakes lose their stigma and become evidence of progress. The classroom atmosphere shifts from evaluation to exploration and from silence to authentic engagement.

One of my favorite parts of visible thinking activities is watching students wrestle with ideas together. In my dual credit Biology class, one of the most challenging tasks we attempted was modeling and explaining the steps of glycolysis. For anyone who has not thought about glycolysis in a while, it is a complex biological process filled with big words, ten total steps, and many inputs and outputs. It is challenging to say the least.

One year, I taught a particularly advanced group of students who fully embraced active learning and took great pride in their knowledge. At first, this was fantastic. Or, fantastic until they disagreed. While modeling glycolysis as a team, this group began debating loudly, though never angrily, about what occurred at each step. I, as the facilitator, quietly listened from the side with pride in my heart. It was an authentic example of meaningful learning, both audible and visible. They were thinking out loud, holding their ideas up to scrutiny, defending their reasoning, and pushing one another toward clarity.

Eventually, when they could not reach a consensus, I stepped in and guided them toward the correct sequence. Even so, watching the learning unfold in real time was priceless. This is the type of engagement we have hoped to achieve through the groundwork we laid in each step of this book.

Ultimately, when thinking is visible, feedback becomes immediate and purposeful. Teachers can respond in the moment, and students can see growth in real time. The result is a classroom where learning feels active, collaborative, and alive.

Collaborative Study Guide Review

One of the best indicators of deep learning is the ability to explain something clearly to someone else. Just as dogs reinforce training through repetition and consistency, students strengthen mastery through retrieval and collaboration. A collaborative study guide review transforms test preparation from a solitary, anxious exercise into an active, community driven experience.

When students create study materials together, they engage in one of the most powerful forms of learning: teaching through synthesis. One effective approach is to divide the class into small groups and assign each a section of the content. Students then use that content to generate potential test questions, detailed answers, and brief rationales. We can further support the process by inviting them to include a mix of question types such as conceptual, application, and critical thinking so the review mirrors the complexity of the actual assessment.

Once groups have built their question sets, it is a good idea to rotate them. Have each new group answer the previous team's questions, adding notes or revisions along the way. This exchange turns the study guide into a living document, a shared product of collective understanding. By the time the final version is published on the learning platform or shared in class, it represents the combined reasoning of the entire group.

In addition, assigning roles can keep the process structured and purposeful. A writer records questions, a checker verifies accuracy, an explainer clarifies reasoning, and a skeptic challenges gaps in understanding. Rotating these roles ensures every student contributes while also strengthening their metacognitive awareness.

Ultimately, the power of collaborative review lies in its authenticity. Students take ownership because the product serves a meaningful purpose: it helps them and their peers prepare. Further, they realize that studying involves connecting, explaining, and refining. The review serves as an extension of learning rather than the end of it.

Research Spotlight: Why Active Beats Passive

Brain based learning research confirms what experienced teachers instinctively understand: students learn more when they are engaged, moving, and thinking. Active learning engages multiple neural systems at once, including attention, memory, language, motor coordination, and social reasoning, which creates stronger and more durable connections in the brain (GSI Teaching and Resource Center, 2023).

To build on this, when students manipulate, explain, and apply ideas, they transform information into understanding. Learning is not a single event; it is a physiological process of strengthening neural networks. Each time a student recalls a fact, uses it in conversation, or applies it to solve a problem, that network becomes stronger and easier to access. In contrast, passive listening activates fewer regions of the brain and produces weaker retention over time.

Further evidence comes from a landmark study showing that students in lecture-based STEM courses were one and a half times more likely to fail than those who experienced active learning (Freeman et al., 2014). On average, active learning improved exam performance by half a letter grade. The content was the same; the approach was different. Even small instructional shifts such as adding peer discussion, short retrieval activities, or collaborative problem-solving produced measurable gains.

In addition, active learning influences classroom climate. When students engage in discussion, creation, or movement, they feel seen and valued as participants in their own education. This sense of agency strengthens motivation and belonging, both of which are vital to long term success.

Taken together, the science aligns with practice. Participation changes outcomes. Active learning is not a trend or a gimmick. It reflects the natural way the brain learns best. When teachers design lessons that invite interaction and reflection, they transform learning from an act of endurance into an act of joy. Students finish class not exhausted, but fulfilled. That is the kind of tired that makes tails wag.

Practical Strategies for Setting Students Up for Success

Creating a productive learning environment is essential. Much like giving a dog the right job prevents unwanted habits, thoughtful planning and intentional structure set students up for calm focus and steady engagement. The strategies below support a classroom where students have clear direction, meaningful roles, and the conditions needed to thrive.

1. **Plan in Purposeful Intervals**
   Structure lessons in short segments that balance input, interaction, and reflection. Think 10–15-minute bursts of focus, followed by active engagement. Use visible timers and transition cues to signal movement and keep energy steady.
2. **Chunk and Scaffold Learning**
   Present complex concepts in manageable steps. Offer partial notes, examples, or graphic organizers early, then gradually remove supports as students gain confidence. Visible progress builds persistence.
3. **Appoint Student Leaders**
   Designate one leader per group to receive instructions directly from you, then reteach to their peers. Rotate roles so every student experiences leadership and collaboration. This promotes independence and accountability.
4. **Use Movement with Purpose**
   Build transitions that require students to stand, share, or move. Gallery walks, think-and-switch discussions, and learning stations refresh attention while reinforcing content. Keep movement structured and time-bound to maintain focus.
5. **Make Thinking Visible**
   Provide whiteboards, chalk markers, or digital tools for quick responses and visual explanations. When students display their thinking, misconceptions surface early and understanding deepens.

6. **Keep the Space Flexible**
   Arrange desks to match the activity. Circles and clusters invite conversation; open lanes support movement. A flexible room layout saves time and reduces friction.

Closing Reflection

When a dog has spent the day exploring, training, and working alongside its handler, it settles easily. There is no restlessness, no mischief, only the quiet contentment that comes from having purpose and direction. The same calm fills a classroom where students have been actively engaged in meaningful learning. When their curiosity has been sparked, their voices heard, and their energy guided, they too settle, not from exhaustion but from fulfillment.

Active instruction transforms the tone of a room. Instead of managing behaviors, we manage momentum. Instead of asking for attention, we design for it. Every interval of movement, every turn to talk, and every moment of creation keeps the mind alive and the heart connected.

This approach prioritizes balance rather than entertainment or constant motion. It requires knowing when to guide, when to step back, and when to let students lead. Success in learning, much like success in training, grows from clarity, consistency, and connection. When we plan with these principles in mind, the classroom hums with a quiet confidence that no rule or consequence could ever produce.

I was reminded of this the day Bear finally got his rainy-day walk, when restless energy transformed into calm satisfaction with just the right amount of challenge and purpose. Our classrooms work the same way. A well-designed lesson gives students what Bear found that day: direction, purpose, and the peace that follows meaningful effort. That is the kind of tired that makes tails wag, the kind of day that reminds us why we teach.

Reflection Questions

1. Think about the flow of a typical lesson in your classroom. Where could you add short intervals of movement or interaction to keep students actively engaged?

2. How might you adjust your lesson pacing using the **Age Plus Two** guideline to match students' natural attention spans?
3. How do you make student thinking visible? What new strategies could you try to help students see their own progress and understanding more clearly?
4. Reflect on your classroom setup. Does the physical arrangement of your space support the kind of learning you want to see? What small changes could make collaboration and movement easier?

Try This Tomorrow

Stand, Share, Switch

- Choose one meaningful question from the lesson that requires more than recall.
- Ask students to write their response on a small whiteboard or notecard.
- After a minute of thinking time, have students stand and find a partner who is not seated near them.
- Each student shares their response, listens to their partner, then trades boards or cards.
- On your cue, students find a new partner and repeat the process.
- After two or three rounds, bring the class together and invite a few volunteers to share ideas they encountered that differed from their own.
- Use the brief discussion to reveal misconceptions, highlight new perspectives, and reinforce that learning is social, active, and engaging.

Chapter 10: Correction – The Least Invasive Approach

We are the leaders of the pack.

In every classroom, students look to us for direction, stability, and safety. Whether they realize it or not, they are constantly reading our tone, our body language, and our reactions. Our presence signals what kind of day it will be. Will this be a space of calm or chaos, connection or control? The answer begins with us.

Leadership in the classroom goes beyond authority and reaches toward steadiness. It means showing students that boundaries and care can coexist, and that expectations and empathy can work together rather than compete. When we model composure, we teach emotional regulation far more effectively than any explanation of behavior ever could.

Early in my teaching journey, I watched a mentor embody this truth in a way I will never forget. During my student teaching, a seventh-grade boy named Joey was doing everything he could to disrupt the lesson: talking loudly, dropping supplies, and trying to make his classmates laugh. When class ended, the teacher called him over to talk and invited me to observe. I braced for a stern reprimand. Instead, she spoke gently. *"Joey, you know I like you, and I am always proud of how hard you try to stay focused. What happened today?"*

Her tone was calm, her posture open. There was no anger and no lecture, only genuine curiosity. Joey's shoulders dropped. He admitted he had argued with his mom that morning and had come to class still upset. The conversation ended quietly, not with punishment, but with understanding.

Eighteen years later, I still remember that moment. It reshaped how I viewed classroom management. True correction begins with composure. When we lead with calm, we lead with clarity. Students grow not through our control, but through our consistency and care.

The Calm in the Chaos

Every classroom has a pulse. Some days it beats steadily, and other days it races. There are moments when energy swells or frustration sparks, and in those moments, our presence sets the tone. Students follow our lead more than our words. When we steady ourselves, we steady the room.

Emotional regulation is one of the most powerful, yet least discussed, aspects of classroom management. As previously mentioned, research on emotional contagion has shown that emotions can be transferred from one person to another through subtle cues such as facial expression, tone, and posture (Hatfield et al., 1994). In a classroom, this means that a teacher's calm can literally lower students' stress levels, while frustration or tension can raise them. Students, particularly adolescents, are highly attuned to our cues. They mirror not only our mood but also our method of handling challenge.

Calm is not passive. It is an intentional practice of regulating our own emotions before responding to theirs. When we respond rather than react, we model the self-control we hope students will learn to practice. This kind of composure does not ignore misbehavior. Instead, it allows us to address the behavior without damaging the relationship.

In addition, teaching through calm reshapes the classroom climate. Studies on teacher affect show that a positive emotional tone predicts greater student engagement, motivation, and achievement (Jennings & Greenberg, 2009; Marzano et al., 2003). When students perceive the classroom as emotionally safe, their brains shift from a state of defense to one of openness and curiosity. Learning requires vulnerability, the willingness to risk confusion, error, and growth. Calm provides the safety that makes that risk possible.

Ultimately, when tensions rise, students are not watching for control. They are watching for stability. They want to know whether they can trust us to stay grounded when things get hard. Our calm tells them that no matter what happens, the classroom remains a safe place to land.

Don't Grab the Rope

Every teacher knows the moment when a challenge hangs in the air. The eye roll, the sarcastic comment, or the quiet refusal that dares a response. In that instant, it can feel as if a rope appears between teacher and student, waiting for someone to take hold. The student tugs gently, testing our reaction, and everything in us wants to pull back. The secret to managing these moments is not to drop the rope once it is tight. It is to never pick it up at all.

A professor once gave me that advice early in my career: *"Don't grab the rope."* At the time, it sounded almost too simple. Yet years of experience have proven how wise it is. When a student tests boundaries, they are not searching for partnership; they are seeking control. If we react in frustration, we take the bait and enter a contest no one wins.

Power struggles may look like they are about rules or respect, but underneath, they are driven by emotion. The moment we step into a tug of war, we send the message that our authority is something to be defended rather than something we already possess. True authority is steady, grounded, and confident, and it does not need to prove itself.

I once had a colleague who learned this lesson in the hardest way. She was a veteran teacher nearing retirement who had grown frustrated by what she saw as a lack of discipline in her freshman class. Each day her patience thinned until she began yelling, losing her composure, and eventually breaking into tears. Her students, sensing her frustration, began pushing her on purpose. They found it entertaining to make her angry and even to make her cry. Soon they were bragging in other teachers' classrooms about who had come closest. It was cruel, no doubt, but it also revealed something important: she had lost her credibility. By letting her emotions take over, she had taught them that her classroom was not a safe place to learn.

That experience has stayed with me. It reminded me that the moment we lose our cool, we lose our influence. When we react emotionally, the focus shifts from behavior to conflict, and the lesson students receive centers on control rather than respect or growth.

Research supports what experienced teachers have long observed. Jones and Jones (2021) note that teachers who maintain composed authority while avoiding emotional confrontation preserve both classroom order and student dignity. Kohn (1996) argues that control creates compliance, while collaboration builds commitment. When we refuse to grab the rope, we shift the goal from winning a struggle to guiding a learner.

In practice, this begins with learning to pause before responding. Silence often communicates confidence more clearly than words. It also means addressing the behavior privately rather than publicly, because public correction can turn the moment into a performance. In addition, responding with curiosity rather than irritation by asking *"What is going on?"* instead of *"Why did you do that?"* encourages reflection rather than defensiveness.

Choosing not to grab the rope does not mean overlooking behavior or lowering expectations. It means correcting without confrontation and maintaining authority without anger. When students realize we will not match their emotion, the rope loses its power. Calm cannot be manipulated.

In time, students learn something deeper. They learn that power struggles offer no real power at all. When we refuse to grab the rope, we preserve our authority and protect relationships. Steadiness becomes the guide, and the classroom remains a place where learning, not conflict, takes center stage.

The Power of Presence and Proximity

A teacher's presence can fill a room long before a single word is spoken. Students notice the way we enter, the steadiness of our voice, and the confidence in our posture. They read our expressions and body language more quickly than they process our instructions. Our presence is, in many ways, our first and most constant classroom management tool.

Research on teacher nonverbal behavior consistently shows that proximity, posture, and tone influence student engagement and behavior more than verbal correction (Simonsen et al., 2008). Composed authority is communicated through subtle cues such as a pause in instruction, a slow walk toward an off-task group, a quiet look that says, *"I see you."* These cues convey both awareness and leadership without interrupting the flow of learning.

In practice, proximity is one of the simplest and most effective strategies for prevention. Moving through the room naturally signals that attention and care are shared equally among all students. It communicates that the teacher is both present and in command of the space. A quiet walk toward chatter, a gentle hand on a desk, or standing near a distracted group often restores focus more effectively than verbal redirection ever could.

Body language also shapes the emotional tone of the classroom. An open stance communicates safety and confidence, while crossed arms or clenched hands can send a message of frustration even when our words are kind. The aim is to appear approachable, yet firm and consistent. We can correct behavior without confrontation simply by adjusting how we position ourselves.

Voice matters as well. A steady tone commands more respect than volume ever will. The most powerful words are often spoken softly rather than loudly. When a teacher raises their voice, it signals loss of control; when we lower it, students instinctively quiet down to listen.

Ultimately, the best management rarely looks like management. It looks like quiet confidence, steady movement, and intentional presence. It is the teacher who corrects behavior with a look instead of a lecture and who reclaims attention with a pause rather than a shout.

When we master presence and proximity, we guide the room's energy with subtle cues that protect both learning and dignity. In time, students come to see calm as a quiet kind of strength.

Behavior is Not the Student

Correction should reflect our belief that every student is capable of learning, growing, and doing better. When students make poor choices, their actions can feel personal, especially when they seem directed at us. Yet discipline has the greatest impact when we respond with perspective instead of emotion. In this way, we can hold students accountable and still preserve the relationship.

When we treat behavior as *something a student does rather than who they are*, we create space for growth. Students learn that mistakes are temporary and that they have the power to make different choices next time. This mindset builds trust and encourages reflection instead of defensiveness. It also models emotional maturity, showing students how to own their actions without internalizing shame.

Restorative approaches to discipline reinforce this philosophy. They emphasize repairing harm, rebuilding trust, and restoring a sense of belonging rather than assigning blame (Amstutz & Mullet, 2015). In this process, the teacher becomes a partner who helps students understand the impact of their behavior and take responsibility in meaningful ways. As a result, accountability becomes an act of respect as well as a tool for learning.

Language choices also matter. Phrases such as *"I like you, but I don't like this behavior"* reassure students that their value is not defined by their actions. Asking *"What happened?"* instead of *"Why did you do that?"* encourages reflection without accusation. Our words shape how students perceive both the correction and themselves.

Students who already question whether they belong often interpret discipline as rejection. Tone, posture, and follow up can either deepen that belief or dismantle it. When we end a conversation with reassurance such as *"I know you can do better"* or *"Let us start fresh tomorrow,"* we help students see possibility rather than disappointment. They leave knowing the relationship remains intact.

Correction handled with empathy strengthens relationships. When students recognize that accountability comes from care, they learn to trust the process. They see expectations as a sign or belief in their potential.

At its core, classroom management comes back to relationships. When we approach missteps with steadiness and respect, we remind students that they are more than the choices they make. Growth, belonging, and learning remain within reach.

Three Levels of Correction

Correction works best when it is consistent, respectful, and scaled to the situation. Not every behavior requires the same response. Some moments call for a gentle cue, others for a private conversation, and occasionally for more formal accountability. The goal is to guide behavior without damaging trust.

The following framework provides a progression of responses that preserve dignity while addressing the issue. It is not a rigid formula, but a guiding mindset. We begin with the least invasive approach and increase intensity only when needed. In this way, each step keeps the focus on growth and responsibility instead of control.

Level One: Gentle Redirection

The first response should be light, quick, and calm. A subtle cue or reminder often stops a behavior before it grows. We can make eye contact, move closer, or offer a brief comment such as *"Let's refocus"* or *"I need your attention."* In these moments, we address the behavior, not the student's character, and then move on. The interaction should be so brief that it does not interrupt instruction or draw unnecessary attention.

This level communicates awareness and consistency. Students learn that expectations are steady and predictable. They also learn that we address issues quickly and respectfully, without public embarrassment or frustration.

Level Two: Reflective Conversation

If a behavior repeats or begins to affect the learning environment, we can step aside for a short one-on-one conversation. Our tone should be curious, not punitive. We ask what is going on and listen. Many times, the simple act of being heard is enough to defuse tension.

We begin with empathy: *"I've noticed you've been distracted lately, which isn't like you. What's making it hard to stay focused?"* Allow silence to work in your favor. Students often fill the space with reflection. We end with reassurance: *"I know you can turn this around. Let's both reset and start again."*

In the end, reflective conversations teach responsibility through dialogue, not confrontation. They remind students that behavior involves choices and that they have control over what happens next.

Level Three: Restorative Accountability

When a behavior becomes persistent despite earlier conversations, the next step is to pair accountability with a small, purposeful consequence. The goal is not punishment but reflection, a moment that helps the student understand how their actions affect others and gives them a chance to repair it.

To support this, the consequence should match the behavior. If a student consistently arrives late and disrupts others, we can ask them to remain for a brief moment after class to discuss how they can enter more smoothly next time. If materials are mishandled, we may ask the student to help organize supplies before the next activity. If class time has been wasted, we can assign a short reflection on how the behavior impacted learning. These responses keep the correction connected to the context.

What matters most is tone. We speak calmly and clearly about the expectation, the reason for the consequence, and the opportunity to reset. For example, *"I need you to stay for a minute after class so we can talk about how to make the start of next period go more smoothly"* is firm but respectful. Students learn that actions carry natural outcomes, not arbitrary punishments.

In addition, this level focuses on restoration, not removal. It allows the student to take responsibility while staying part of the learning community. When consequences are logical and delivered with consistency and care, they reinforce fairness and strengthen credibility.

At its heart, the most effective correction is the one that ends with growth. A student who leaves knowing how to make it right walks away with more than discipline; they walk away with dignity.

Beyond the Three Tiers

Most schools define a three-tiered approach to managing behavior. The first response is a gentle reminder, the second a private conversation, and the third a formal step such as contacting parents or referring the student to the office. On paper, this process seems logical. However, in practice, it can easily undermine the very relationships that make classroom management effective.

At first, calling home may seem like the natural next step, but it does not always produce the outcome we hope for. Some parents immediately support the teacher's authority, but others may question it, contradict it, or unintentionally weaken it. Research on teacher–parent dynamics shows that when parents view the teacher's role as less authoritative, the student's respect for that authority also declines (Velez et al., 2022). The result can be confusion, resentment, or even escalation. Instead of solving the issue, the call home can fracture the trust between student and teacher.

When the next step becomes a referral to the office, a similar pattern often repeats. Many deans and administrators operate from restorative practice models, which begin with relationship-building conversations. While well-intentioned, these interactions can feel like a reward to a student seeking attention or escape. A teacher's authority can be quietly eroded when a student learns that misbehavior leads to a more relaxed environment or a sympathetic listener. Once that dynamic is established, some students begin to chase the referral. They push limits, hoping to be sent out because it feels easier than staying in.

These cycles are not about malice or manipulation; they are about reinforcement. The student learns that misbehavior removes them from discomfort, while the teacher learns that authority can be undermined by inconsistent follow-through. Research on administrative intervention supports this concern. When teachers' classroom management is second-guessed or not reinforced by leadership, students perceive the teacher as powerless, and misbehavior increases (Fordham Institute, 2022).

This is why I try to keep correction within my own classroom whenever possible. The more challenges we can solve together, the stronger the relationship becomes. Holding students accountable in the same space where the learning happens teaches them that discipline is part of growth, not a separate event. It shows them that they can recover, repair, and rejoin the group without losing belonging.

When the three tiers seem to fail, the solution is not necessarily to move up the chain. It is often to move deeper into the relationship. A calm conversation, a small reflective consequence, or a simple *"Let's try again tomorrow"* communicates belief in the student's capacity to improve. Authority is not maintained by handing a student off to someone else. It is strengthened when we stay, lead, and keep the bond intact.

Rebuilding From Inside the Classroom

When behavior persists despite our best efforts, the answer is rarely a louder response or a higher authority. More often, it is steadiness.

Maintaining positive rapport with high expectations does far more to repair behavior than sending students out or calling home. Each time we solve a problem within the classroom, we strengthen both the relationship and our credibility.

To support this, correction should never become a contest of power. Instead, we gently tighten the boundaries while keeping encouragement close at hand. Students should always feel there is a clear way back. When they begin to show improvement, even in small ways, we name it quietly and sincerely. A short note, a brief email, or a simple *"I noticed your effort today"* communicates belief more effectively than any consequence.

This is also where language matters. I am careful to separate the student from the behavior. When a student hears, *"I like you, but I need you to make a better choice,"* the message is clear: the behavior needs to change, but the relationship is safe. That single distinction often determines whether a student feels defensive or determined to do better.

In addition, I also work to keep consequences framed as part of learning, not punishment. When students see that a consequence is simply the next step in repairing the moment, it loses its sting. My tone matters as much as my words, I might say, *"I wish you didn't have this consequence, but it's here because of the choice that was made. Let's take care of it and move forward."* In this way, the consequence becomes something to complete, not something to resent.

Keeping discipline within the classroom teaches students that accountability and belonging can coexist. When they see that we remain steady, consistent, and compassionate through their mistakes, they learn to regulate themselves. The path back to trust becomes visible.

Recognize the Positive

Correction does not end when behavior changes. In many ways, that is where the real work begins. Once a student starts making better choices, our next responsibility is to notice. Recognition is how we signal that effort matters and that growth never goes unseen.

One of my favorite examples of this came on a spring day that could have easily turned into frustration. Each year, our school took the freshman class on a field trip during standardized testing for the upper grades. By the time buses returned, there were about forty-five minutes left in the day. One year, only half of my students came back to class. Where the others went was anyone's guess. It was a school-wide issue, but in that moment, I could only control my response.

Rather than dwell on the missing students, I focused on the students who did what was expected. I wanted to send a message that following through mattered and that reliability would always be noticed. Those who returned were allowed to relax with friends, catch up on other assignments, or simply enjoy a brief moment of freedom. Before they left, I handed each one a hot pink **Thank You Slip**, bright enough to draw attention. Each note carried the same reward: one late assignment, forgiven without penalty.

The next morning, the ripple was clear. Students who had skipped the last class wanted to know what the slips were for. Without anger or lecture, the message had spread. Doing the right thing had been recognized through appreciation rather than consequence.

This is the quiet power of reinforcement. It teaches through modeling and acknowledgement. Positive reinforcement means being just as intentional about recognizing progress as we are about correcting mistakes. Research on schoolwide positive behavior supports this practice. Consistent, authentic recognition of appropriate behavior builds stronger engagement and reduces disruptions over time (Sugai & Horner, 2002). The key is sincerity. Students know when praise is genuine and when it is routine.

When we take time to notice effort, whether it is a chronically late student arriving on time, a typically talkative student staying focused, or a reluctant learner contributing, we remind them that growth is visible. The goal is not to create a reward system. Instead, it is to sustain a culture of respect where positive behavior feels seen and valued.

Recognition and correction work together. Correction shows students where boundaries are, and recognition shows them why those boundaries matter. When both are done with authenticity, classroom management becomes less about control and more about community.

Balancing Empathy and Expectations

Empathy without expectation breeds chaos, and expectation without empathy breeds resentment. Effective classroom management lives in the space between the two. It is the place where students know they are cared for and where that care comes with boundaries that protect everyone's right to learn.

This balance begins with how we see our role. We are not just content experts; we are emotional leaders. Students take their cues from us, not only in what we say, but in how we react when things go wrong. A teacher's ability to stay composed under pressure communicates security more powerfully than any consequence ever could. Research on emotional intelligence in teaching shows that our emotional regulation directly shapes classroom climate (Hargreaves, 1998). Calm breeds calm.

Empathy invites understanding, and expectation provides structure. Both are necessary. When a student falls short, empathy asks, *"What's behind this behavior?"* while expectation says, *"You are still responsible for your choices."* The goal is not to choose between compassion and accountability, but to intertwine them so that each strengthens the other.

Furthermore, students read fairness faster than they read rules. When they sense that we hold them to high standards because we believe in their potential, they respond with greater effort and trust. Conversely, when empathy turns into permissiveness, they lose both direction and respect. Boundaries and kindness work best when they move together.

Holding this balance requires steady reflection. Some days, empathy must lead, and on others, expectation must guide. The art of teaching lies in knowing which is needed, and when. Over time, we come to see that consistency and care are partners in presence. What students remember most is how we handled their hardest moments, whether we steadied or shamed, reacted or responded. When they witness empathy and expectation working together, they learn that strength and kindness can exist in the same breath, and that both can lead.

Research Spotlight: Teacher Actions Matter Most

Everything in this book, from routines to relationships, rests on a simple truth confirmed again and again by research: what teachers do every day in their classrooms has the greatest impact on student behavior and learning.

Research indicates that teachers' classroom management practices influence student achievement more than any other factor within a school's control. In fact, teacher actions in the classroom have roughly *twice the impact* on student outcomes as schoolwide policies or administrative interventions (Marzano et al., 2003). This means how we greet students, respond to disruption, and manage momentum holds far more power to shape learning than any external system or consequence.

These findings underscore why calm correction, relational discipline, and classroom-based accountability work. When we keep redirection between ourselves and the student, we preserve the connection that makes teaching effective. Strong teacher–student relationships create trust, and trust opens the door to influence.

In addition, the research emphasizes that effective classroom management grows from prevention and presence. Clear expectations, predictable routines, and timely private redirection support both order and emotional safety (Marzano et al., 2003). These same principles echo through every chapter of this book.

When we respond with consistency and care, we model the behavior we hope to cultivate. The evidence is clear. Classrooms thrive not because of rules posted on a wall, but because of relationships built within them and the way we tend to those relationships when challenges arise.

Practical Strategies to Correct with Care

Correction is most effective when it protects trust while guiding students back on track. The following strategies support firm boundaries delivered with empathy and steadiness.

1. **Start Small, Stay Consistent**
   Address misbehavior early and quietly. A brief cue or change in proximity prevents escalation and shows awareness of every student, every time.

2. **Keep It Private**
   Correction delivered in confidence preserves dignity and keeps the class focused on learning, not spectacle. Public shaming breeds resistance; private redirection builds respect.

3. **Match Consequence to Context**
   Let the response connect directly to the behavior. For example, require a minute after class for repeated lateness, ask the student to reorganize materials that were misused, or assign a short reflection for lost learning time. Logical consequences teach accountability better than arbitrary ones.

4. **Acknowledge the Turnaround**
   When students improve, say so. Authentic acknowledgment, such as *"I noticed your effort today"* reinforces growth and helps students recognize their own progress.

5. **Separate Person from Behavior**
   Always speak to the action, not the character. *"You're capable of better choices"* invites growth; *"You're disrespectful"* invites defensiveness.

6. **Hold Steady Emotionally**
   Your composure is the anchor of the classroom. Take a breath before responding. Steady, consistent tone communicates safety and confidence.

7. **End Every Correction with Reconnection**
   A brief *"We're good"* or *"Fresh start tomorrow"* restores belonging and reminds students that mistakes are moments, not identities.

Closing Reflection

Classroom management is not measured by the absence of misbehavior but by the presence of trust. It is the ability to redirect energy without breaking trust, to correct behavior while keeping connection. These same ideas follow me home each day, where I see them play out in real time.

As Bear, our new rescue, acclimates to our home, we have learned a valuable lesson about behavior and belonging. If Bella barks and becomes uneasy, Bear immediately follows suit. He is not fearful by nature, but he mirrors her energy and reacts to her tone. To calm him, I had to start by modifying her behavior.

Rather than punish the barking, I chose to redirect it. I ordered a small beeping device that emits a brief sound to catch attention. Each time it beeps, I call, *"Come to me!"* and reward both dogs when they respond. In only a few weeks, Bella has started to pause when she's about to bark, correct herself, and come running with excitement for her treat. Bear follows, calmer and more confident each time. The correction is consistent, the reinforcement is kind, and the chaos has faded.

That small, daily practice reminds me that the same truths hold in our classrooms. Change happens through consistency and connection. Correction without shame builds trust, and trust builds confidence. Whether it is a barking dog or a restless student, behavior shifts when the leader models being calm, gives clear direction, and follows through with care.

In the end, that is what correction is really about. Not compliance. Not power. But guiding others toward self-control through our own steadiness. When we lead with both expectation and empathy, students, or even dogs, like Bella and Bear, learn that steady is safe, correction is fair, and growth is possible.

Reflection Questions

1. Which level of correction (gentle redirection, reflective conversation, restorative accountability) feels most natural for you, and which requires more intentional practice?
2. How might you ensure your corrections preserve dignity while maintaining high expectations?
3. Think of a student whose behavior once frustrated you. How could a focus on relationship rather than referral have changed the outcome?
4. What language shifts could help you separate the student from the behavior in future corrections?
5. How can you quietly reinforce positive change so students feel both seen and motivated to continue improving?

Try This Tomorrow

Correction Cards

- Keep a small stack of blank index cards or sticky notes at your desk.
- When a student turns a behavior around, such as arriving on time, staying on task, or helping a peer, write a brief thank you or acknowledgment.
- Place the note on the student's desk before the end of class.
- Notice how this quick, tangible recognition reinforces the behaviors you want to grow.
- Reflect on how small moments of recognition build trust and reduce the need for correction over time.

Chapter 11: Teaching Old Dogs New Tricks – The Five R's of Classroom Renewal

It is definitely harder to disallow something you used to permit, for both dogs and students.

Prior to Liberty's arrival in our home, Bella had full run of the house, including our second floor. She didn't sleep there; she just liked to follow us when we went upstairs to grab something from the bedroom or fold a load of laundry. It was harmless enough, or so I thought.

When Liberty joined our family, she had already worked hard to master the stairs leading from our main level down to the patio. That was no small feat for an older, heavier dog, and although her balance and confidence improved, we could see that transversing another flight of stairs would be too much strain on her hips. To protect her mobility, we decided that neither dog would go upstairs any longer.

Bella did not appreciate this change. The first few days were full of whines, dramatic sighs, and the occasional attempt to sneak up a few steps before being called back down. I could practically hear her saying, *"But you used to let me!"* And she was right; I had. Which made the correction all the harder.

Still, through consistency and patience, she adapted. Over time, she stopped testing the rule and began waiting calmly at the bottom, watching us from her new "post" with quiet acceptance. The truth is, retraining a behavior, whether canine or human, takes humility on both sides. I had to admit that I'd been inconsistent, and Bella had to learn that boundaries can change.

As I stood at the top of the stairs one evening, watching her wag her tail in understanding rather than frustration, I thought about how similar this is to the classroom. Sometimes, we allow things to slip, small behaviors that seem harmless at first; yet before long, they climb the staircase unchecked. When we finally decide to set the boundary again, the pushback comes. Nevertheless, it is possible to reset. It just requires honesty, clarity, and patience.

Students, like Bella, may not like change at first. Even so, most will come to understand that our decision comes from a desire to make the learning environment better for everyone. Every teacher encounters a moment when the classroom slips off course, whether due to a few late assignments, quiet side conversations, or a general sense of imbalance. Sometimes the cause is external, like mounting academic pressure or shifting social dynamics. Other times, it is internal: the routines we allowed to loosen or expectations we stopped enforcing.

Fortunately, the good news is that just as we can train a new behavior in old dogs, we can also reset our classrooms. For the classroom, the process begins with honesty. When we acknowledge to our students that something is not working, we invite them into a partnership to improve it. Transparency builds trust, and trust opens the door for change.

Research supports this approach. When teachers take the time to pause, reflect, and reset, classrooms not only regain structure but also rebuild emotional safety and engagement. As it turns out, resetting isn't just a strategy; it's an evidence-based practice.

Research Spotlight: The Power of a Classroom Reset

When a classroom starts to drift off balance, an intentional reset can do more than restore order. It can rebuild trust and reengage students in learning. Recent research supports the idea that teachers who pause with purpose to reset expectations, routines, and norms foster stronger and more resilient classroom climates.

Benner and colleagues (2022) examined the Classroom Reset Program, a structured intervention designed to help teachers reestablish norms when behavior issues escalate. Their findings showed that guided resets improved student engagement, decreased disruptions, and increased teacher confidence in managing behavior. The researchers emphasized that resets are most effective when they combine clear expectations, positive reinforcement, and opportunities for reflection, which are principles echoed throughout this chapter.

Moreover, practical research and educator reflections align with these findings. For instance, the Social Emotional Teacher (2023) suggests that a midyear reset should follow steps such as revisiting expectations, reinforcing positive behavior, and integrating social-emotional supports.

Similarly, Napolitan and Bender (2024), as well as, Marye (2024) highlight that natural breaks, such as holidays or the start of a new term, create ideal moments for this recalibration. These resets, they note, not only reduce off-task behavior but also strengthen the emotional safety students feel within the classroom.

Taken together, the research affirms what teachers often sense intuitively. A classroom reset is not an admission of failure. Instead, it is an act of leadership grounded in the belief that both teachers and students can grow, adapt, and begin again with clarity and care.

Revisit

Revisiting is the first step toward rebuilding classroom balance, and it works best when introduced right after a holiday or extended break. The process begins with honesty, first with ourselves and then with our students. When a class climate begins to drift, it rarely happens overnight. Most often, it is the result of gradual leniency, small exceptions, or expectations we quietly allowed to fade.

The most important part of revisiting is reflection. We can begin by asking ourselves which routines, procedures, or rules are still serving our students and which have become unnecessary or even counterproductive. Just because a rule appeared earlier in this book or worked beautifully in a previous class does not mean it still fits our current environment. Every class moves to its own rhythm, and when we recognize and adjust to that rhythm, we demonstrate empathy and care.

When we are ready to bring students into the process, we should approach it openly. We might say, *"I have been thinking about our classroom routines and how we can make them work better for everyone. Let's talk about why we do things the way we do."* For example, we can ask, *"Why do you think we store our book bags up front?"* and let students reason it out: *"For safety, so we can move freely."* When students articulate the reasoning themselves, the rules regain purpose and meaning.

As we go through the list, we can look for one rule or procedure that can be simplified or removed. Throwing something out or modifying it demonstrates flexibility and good faith. Revisiting reminds us that teaching is a shared process. When we reflect openly with our students, we model the kind of learning and growth we hope to see in them.

Reset

Once we have revisited our classroom expectations together, we move directly into the reset. This is the moment when reflection turns into visible action. Resetting shows our students that we are not only talking about a fresh start but actively creating one.

The reset should happen in real time, during the same class period as the revisit if possible. After we review the rules and routines, we can physically change the environment to mark the shift by adjusting seating, reorganizing groups, or updating materials. The movement itself communicates that something new is beginning and that the classroom has intentionally shifted from where we left it before the break.

Next, we make the reset official by offering a clean slate. We tell our students that all past tardies are erased, all behavioral tiers or documentation are cleared, and everyone begins on equal footing. This act of forgiveness and renewal communicates that no one is defined by past choices and that growth is always possible.

In addition, the reset also renews our mindset as educators. It allows us to release frustration and reengage with calm purpose. Resetting is about creating the conditions where learning can begin again with clarity and trust.

Restart

After we have revisited and reset, we move into the restart. This is where energy and connection return. A restart shifts attention from structure to community, moving us from reflection to enthusiasm.

To build on the momentum already generated, the restart should take place in the same class period as the other two steps, rounding out the experience with a sense of shared optimism. Once the rules have been revisited and the slate cleared, we can bring joy and momentum back into the room. This is where a reset jackpot, borrowed from dog training, becomes useful. When focus or motivation has waned, a well-timed burst of reward can interrupt disengagement and reawaken participation. In our classrooms, that reset jackpot might take many forms: bringing in donuts to mark a fresh start, showing a short film, allowing students to work with a preferred partner for the day, permitting earbuds during independent work, or even offering a "free" day to catch up on work. These small celebrations restore energy and signal that while expectations remain high, the classroom is also a place where learning can feel productive and joyful.

Restarting helps our students associate renewed effort with positive emotion. It also helps us rediscover our own enthusiasm for teaching. When we model energy, warmth, and curiosity, students reflect that energy back to us, and the classroom feels alive again. However, renewal fades without continued attention. The real challenge comes after the restart, which involves maintaining that new energy once the novelty wears off. Sustaining the environment we have worked to rebuild requires consistent effort, intentional language, and emotional awareness.

Just as Bella resisted when her upstairs privileges were revoked, we can expect a bit of pushback from our students when expectations shift. Change, even positive change, often meets resistance. Students may test the new boundaries or express frustration as they adjust to the updated expectations in the room. We can anticipate it, accept it as part of the process, and meet it with the same tools that helped us rebuild in the first place: patience, humor, clear communication, connectedness, and compassion.

We set the emotional current of the room every day. When we arrive with optimism, our students feel it. When we enter weary or frustrated, they feel that too. Attitudes are contagious, and as teachers, ours tends to spread the fastest. If we model curiosity, gratitude, and patience, students mirror those same qualities in how they interact with us and one another.

To continue nurturing a positive climate, we must guard the atmosphere we worked so hard to rebuild. That begins with how we frame challenges. Rather than saying, *"This will be hard,"* we can say, *"This will stretch us,"* or *"This will show how much we have grown."* The phrasing we choose shapes how students approach each task and how they view themselves as learners.

We can also catch negativity early. When complaining, cynicism, or resistance start to surface, we redirect it with humor, encouragement, or gratitude. A quick acknowledgment of effort, a light comment that eases tension, or a simple *"thank you for sticking with it"* can stop negativity before it spreads. The goal is not to silence emotion, but to steer it toward learning and connection.

We maintain momentum by remaining passionate about our subject and transparent about why we teach it. When we express appreciation for our role in our students' lives, we humanize the classroom. Sometimes, simply saying, *"This is my job, and I love my job. Let me know when and how I can help,"* reminds students that we are partners in their success.

As Roy T. Bennett (2020) reminds us, *"We cannot control the behavior of others, but we can always choose how we respond to it."* Our response sets the emotional climate for everything that follows.

Maintaining this balance also means managing our feedback intentionally. Jones and Jones (2021) suggest that teachers should aim for at least three positive interactions for every one corrective comment. Some research even indicates a five-to-one ratio is most effective in minimizing disruptive behavior. This means that between 75 and 83 percent of our daily interactions should be positive. That ratio may seem ambitious, but it reflects the reality that encouragement is not a luxury in classroom management; it is the foundation of it.

When we manage the classroom in a way that prevents negative behaviors from overshadowing learning, we protect both individual students and the collective classroom experience. Our goal is not perfection; it is to cultivate an environment where students feel safe, motivated, and capable of growth.

Reflect and Repair

As teachers, we tend to be naturally reflective. Each school year gives us a clean slate, a chance to reconsider what worked, what did not, and what we might do differently next time. Reflection is not limited to August planning or May wrap-ups; it can happen midyear, midweek, or even mid-lesson. When we pause with intention and consider why things may have shifted off course, we create opportunities to strengthen the current class climate and learn what to adjust moving forward.

Sometimes, the issue is not our systems or our students; it is connection. Perhaps we started the year with strong rapport, but as state standards, assessments, and other obligations piled up, the moments that once built relationships were quietly replaced by checklists and deadlines. When that happens, behavior often follows. Just like any relationship, student connection requires consistent attention. If it has been a while since we have paused for a lighthearted check-in, a quick emoji one-on-one, or a moment of genuine interest in our students' lives, that may be the reconnection our class truly needs, and it serves as a reminder not to let relationship maintenance fade into the background.

Looking back, I often think about Adam, the student I mentioned in Chapter 1. His story has stayed with me because it reminds me how easy it is to create a behavior we later resent and how much harder it is to undo it. When his witty, out-of-turn comments began, I rewarded them with a smile and lighthearted acknowledgment, thinking I was building a connection. When I realized I had reinforced the wrong behavior, I responded by withdrawing. I ignored him, hoping the problem would fade on its own. But silence communicates too, and what Adam likely heard in my silence was rejection.

If I could go back, I would have taken him aside and admitted that I had mishandled the situation. I would have told him that I appreciated his humor but needed his voice in the right moments. More importantly, I would have found ways to connect with him beyond correction, to ask about his interests, to let him see that I valued him even when his timing missed the mark. What Adam wanted was not attention for disruption, but connection and a sense of belonging. By meeting those needs directly, I could have reshaped our relationship instead of retreating from it.

Moments like that remind us that repairing relationships is just as important as enforcing expectations. When we model humility, students learn that accountability can coexist with care.

Let's Get Real

Even the best classroom management approach cannot magically solve every behavior issue. Social-emotional maturity, home life, and peer relationships shape behavior in ways we simply cannot control. We show up, plan carefully, and give our best, yet there will always be a few who test every ounce of patience we have. Recognizing that truth does not mean giving up; it means acknowledging the limits of what one teacher can carry.

Within those limits, we face one of the hardest questions of all: how much of ourselves can we give to one student without draining the energy that belongs to the rest of the class? Pulling back does not signal a lack of compassion. It reflects the need to preserve our well-being so we can continue supporting everyone. Far too often, we spend unpaid personal time making parent calls in an effort to help, yet many of those conversations shift toward lengthy explanations of the myriad factors influencing a student's behavior, which leaves little time to focus on solutions. To complicate matters further, parent calls can be unpredictable. In the best scenarios, they open doors for teamwork and mutual understanding. In other situations, they unintentionally exacerbate the behavior we hoped to address.

In my nearly two decades of teaching, I have found that parent contact helps about half the time. Since the pandemic, those odds have dropped. Conversations that once fostered partnership now more often escalate frustration rather than resolution. Research supports what many educators have observed. Post COVID studies indicate that increased family stress, communication fatigue, and disrupted routines have complicated the parent teacher dynamic (Garbe et al., 2020). Additional research links heightened family stress to more reactive communication patterns and greater defensiveness during school related conversations (Hertz et al., 2021; Li, 2025; Wiśniewska-Nogaj, 2025). Earlier research on family dynamics offers insight into why these conversations can derail so quickly, as studies of family enhancement of cognitive style suggest that during emotionally charged interactions, parents may unintentionally reinforce a child's interpretation of events rather than challenge or reframe it, particularly in families already experiencing anxiety or stress (Barrett et al., 1996). Thus, when a single, emotionally draining phone call consumes the time that could have supported twenty students and ultimately intensifies the original problem, we must consider whether that approach truly serves our purpose.

We touched on this in the previous chapter, but it bears repeating: referring students to the dean does not always improve behavior. In fact, when a relationship is already strained, those steps can unintentionally make matters worse. A student sent to the office may return more relaxed, feeling understood by a dean's empathy, and sometimes even seeing that attention as a reward. Some will repeat the same behavior just to experience that one-on-one connection again.

Within these constraints, our challenge is to support the one without sacrificing the many. Whenever possible, we keep correction within our own classroom, where trust can be rebuilt in real time. When students learn that accountability happens within the same walls as learning, they understand that consequences are about growth and repair.

Nonetheless, finding that balance is essential. We cannot be everything to everyone, and pretending we can only leads to resentment. Accepting that truth allows us to focus our energy where it matters most: building relationships that sustain learning, creating lessons that engage, and maintaining the steady presence our students rely on.

Furthermore, remaining emotionally objective helps us navigate those moments. We can care deeply while also protecting our energy. We can believe in growth without accepting every burden as our own. Believing in improvement does not mean endless tolerance; it means believing that improvement is possible for our students and for ourselves.

At the end of the day, we cannot control every factor in our students' lives. What we can control is the climate we create for learning. When we approach each day with empathy, curiosity, and hope, we set the tone for growth. The rest, we meet with grace.

Practical Classroom Renewal Strategies

Classroom renewal requires clarity, transparency, and calm consistency. The Five R's offer a structured path back to balance. The strategies below turn each stage into a practical, actionable move.

1. **Revisit with Honesty**
   Pause to examine routines that have drifted. Identify which expectations still serve students and which no longer fit the classroom environment. Invite students into a brief conversation about the purpose behind key routines so meaning becomes shared rather than imposed.

2. **Reset with Visible Change**
   Mark the shift with a concrete action. Rearrange seats, adjust group placements, or tidy communal spaces. Follow with a clean slate that clears past mistakes or infractions. A visible and symbolic reset communicates that a new beginning is underway.

3. **Restart with Positive Energy**
   Reintroduce warmth and momentum. Offer a reset jackpot moment that reignites engagement such as music during transition time, a short collaborative task, or a few minutes to celebrate effort. Restarting connects structure with joy.

4. **Reflect Before Moving Forward**
   Set aside a moment to consider how the room feels after the reset. Ask what is working and what could help sustain the new tone. Reflection encourages students to take ownership of the climate being rebuilt.

5. **Repair Small Disconnects**
   Address lingering tensions quickly and privately. A short, honest conversation can restore trust faster than any consequence. Repairing connections reinforces that classroom management is rooted in relationship, not control.

6. **Protect the Climate of the Classroom**
   Guard the atmosphere by framing challenges with optimism and curiosity. Redirect negativity early with humor, encouragement, or gratitude. A steady emotional presence teaches students how to navigate change with resilience.

Together, these strategies form a blueprint for renewal. They acknowledge the reality of classroom drift while offering a structured and compassionate path back to balance.

Closing Reflection

When I think back to the lessons Bella and Liberty have taught me, I am reminded that every change in behavior begins with trust. Bella's resistance to staying off the stairs was not defiance; it was confusion. She had been allowed before, and now the rule had changed. It took time, patience, and calm consistency before she understood that this new boundary was necessary.

In teaching, the same truth applies. When we change a rule, reset a routine, or admit that something is not working, our students may push back at first. They are testing not only the rule but also our consistency. With time, and with patience, they will see that boundaries exist to protect them and the learning environment.

Each reset we lead, whether at midyear, midweek, or even mid-lesson, reminds us that teaching is an act of continual renewal. Every day offers a new chance to rebuild trust, reaffirm purpose, and rediscover joy in the process. When we revisit, reset, restart, reflect, and repair, we are deepening the connection that makes learning possible.

Reflection Questions

1. When you have sensed your classroom climate drifting, which of the five R's have you tried? How did it go?
2. How do you communicate honesty and care when revisiting expectations with your students?
3. What boundaries protect your energy and keep your teaching sustainable?
4. Think of a time when you had to "reset" a relationship with a student. What worked? What would you do differently now?
5. How might you model reflection and repair so students see that mistakes are a normal part of growth?

Try This Tomorrow

A Mini Revisit

- Choose one procedure or routine that has drifted.
- At the start of class, briefly revisit its purpose with students.
- Ask one question, such as, *"Why do we do this?"* and allow students to restate the reasoning in their own words.
- End with a clean slate, signaling a fresh start for that single routine.

Chapter 12: Tail-Wagging Takeaways – Pack Leader Wrap-Ups

This chapter summarizes the core lessons of the book into one place, a set of pack leader truths to carry forward. We have practiced the routines, built the relationships, and learned to lead with both confidence and care. Strong classroom management grows from structure that holds, relationships that matter, and leadership that remains steady under pressure.

Together, these practices create classrooms where learning feels protected and possible. The Pack Leader Takeaways that follow bring those ideas into focus, while the section on positive training highlights how encouragement and consistency shape lasting behavior. The chapter closes with a final reflection centered on empathy and effort, reminding us that students work hardest for leaders who see them, support them, and believe in their growth. When we lead with consistency and heart, learning follows. When we lead with passion, it spreads.

Pack Leader Takeaway: The First Day Sets the Tone for the Year

The first day of school establishes the patterns that shape everything that follows. What students experience in those opening moments becomes the standard they carry forward. Routines, expectations, and reinforcement communicate stability and care before content ever enters the discussion.

From the outset, explicit procedures create clarity. When expectations are named, shown, and reinforced in the moment, students settle into the learning environment with greater confidence. Assigned seats, entrance routines, listening expectations, and phone systems signal that learning time is protected and purposeful. Further, each procedure communicates that the classroom operates with intention.

Attention functions as powerful currency. The behaviors we notice, respond to, and reinforce are the ones that grow. Subtle, immediate acknowledgment of desired behavior shapes the climate more effectively than public praise or correction. From the very first day, students learn exactly what earns attention and what does not.

Alongside these structures, the teacher's presence anchors the classroom. Students take their cues from steadiness, consistency, and tone. When guidance remains composed, authority holds and trust begins to form. The room feels predictable, secure, and ready for learning.

The first day does more than launch a schedule. It establishes habits. Those habits become the heartbeat of the year ahead.

Pack Leader Takeaway: Predictable Structure Builds Trust

The first week determines the credibility of the tone set on day one. Students watch closely to see if routines hold and expectations remain steady. When structure is reinforced consistently, the classroom begins to feel predictable, and predictability builds trust.

Securing attention is critical. Routines only work when students are tuned in at the right moments. Ensuring focus before giving directions, waiting for eyes and bodies to signal readiness, and refusing to compete with side chatter teaches students that listening matters. When attention is honored, instruction gains weight and routines gain traction.

Consistency communicates reliability. When expectations are enforced the same way each day, the classroom feels steady and fair. Predictable responses reduce boundary testing, lower anxiety, and free students to focus on learning rather than anticipating what might happen next.

Reinforcement shapes the classroom climate early. Quiet, immediate acknowledgment of expected behavior shows students what earns attention. When recognition is steady and equitable, trust grows. Students learn that effort is noticed and that success is possible.

Procedures protect learning time. Clear sequencing, practiced routines, and intentional pacing prevent confusion and preserve instructional flow. Small details, applied consistently, keep learning time intact.

By the end of the first week, students know what to expect and what they can rely on. This predictability builds trust and becomes the quiet assurance that allows learning to commence with confidence.

Pack Leader Takeaway: Developing a Cohesive Pack

The first month determines whether a classroom functions as a collection of individuals or as a cohesive community. This is the point where classroom culture develops. During this phase, students watch to see if expectations hold, if follow-through remains steady, and if relationships extend beyond surface niceties. When consistency continues with genuine care, trust expands into belonging.

Belonging grows when expectations are upheld with steadiness rather than force. During this phase, students test boundaries to confirm reliability. When responses remain predictable and composed, students learn that the classroom is stable and that relationships remain secure even when expectations are enforced.

Community also depends on how students learn to work with one another. Collaboration does not emerge on its own. It must be taught deliberately so students understand what productive group work looks like. Clear norms for interaction, shared responsibility, and accountability define expectations and prevent collaboration from becoming avoidance or imbalance. When collaboration is defined well, students learn that thinking together requires effort, respect, and contribution from everyone.

Intentional structure then supports that collaboration in practice. Defined roles, purposeful grouping, and predictable group locations reduce uncertainty and prevent disengagement. When students know their responsibilities and where they belong, group work runs smoothly and accountability feels fair.

As peer relationships develop through collaborative processes, it strengthens learner independence. When students are taught to rely on one another before turning to the teacher, the classroom shifts from a one-way system to a shared network of learning. Questions circulate, understanding deepens, and students take pride in being resources for one another.

Belonging also extends beyond student interactions. Trust grows strongest when relationships align across students, teachers, and families. When parents feel included and informed early, they engage as partners in the learning process. Furthermore, the shared understanding and mutual respect strengthen the classroom community.

The first month establishes a cohesive pack. When structure holds steady, collaboration is taught, and relationships are nurtured intentionally, the classroom settles into a shared way of working together. In that environment, students learn that they belong, that their contribution matters, and that learning is a collaborative process.

Pack Leader Takeaway: Shaping Classroom Behavior

Behavior in the classroom follows predictable patterns. Students repeat what is reinforced and abandon what is not. This knowledge shifts classroom management from reaction to design, allowing the environment to work for us rather than against us.

Hyperawareness is a critical skill because effective classroom management depends on noticing early signals and responding before small disruptions escalate. Presence, movement, and attention to detail allow teachers to guide behavior proactively.

From there, attention becomes a powerful lever. Where attention is directed teaches students what matters. Inconsistent attention, or attention given to undesirable behaviors, even in small doses, can unintentionally strengthen the very behaviors we want to eliminate. Students continue to test behaviors that occasionally earn a reaction. Vigilance in where attention flows determines what grows.

Every response functions as a consequence. Attention, redirection, silence, and relief all teach students what to expect next. When consequences remain clear and consistent, students connect their choices with predictable outcomes. This clarity reduces confusion and builds confidence.

Reinforcement shapes behavior. Early on, frequent acknowledgment helps students recognize which behaviors matter. As habits form, intermittent reinforcement works best. That variability strengthens behavior, making it more durable. With an unpredictable schedule of reinforcement, students continue meeting expectations even when recognition is not guaranteed. Reinforcement also works through modeling. Students watch one another closely and adjust their behavior based on what they see acknowledged. In this way, expectations spread through example rather than confrontation, and classroom culture strengthens from within.

Be wary of punishment. Punishment has limits. While it may stop behavior in the moment, it rarely teaches what should replace it. Use it sparingly, if at all. Preserving dignity and keeping relationships intact matters most, so punishment should be avoided when reinforcement is possible.

Behavioral psychology does not offer tricks. It offers predictable outcomes through hyperawareness, mindful attention, and deliberate reinforcement. When these elements work together, behavior is teachable, habits stabilize, and classroom culture grows by design rather than chance.

Pack Leader Takeaway: Relationships Strengthen the Pack

Relationships are the most important aspect of classroom management. Routines may establish order, and structure may build trust, but relationships give those systems meaning. When students feel known, respected, and cared for, they are far more willing to engage, persist, and grow.

Care and consistency work together. Strong relationships are not built through permissiveness or popularity, but through steady expectations held with compassion. When students see that boundaries remain firm and fair, they learn that trust does not disappear when guidance is needed. That reliability strengthens connection rather than weakening it.

Meeting emotional needs expands learning capacity. Students carry emotional experiences into the classroom each day, and learning accelerates when those needs are acknowledged. Small, consistent practices that recognize feelings, identities, and experiences communicate that students are valued as people, not just learners. When students feel safe and seen, their willingness to take academic risks increases.

Recognition further strengthens belonging. Using names, making eye contact, and offering specific acknowledgment signals that individuals matter within the group. These moments do more than reinforce behavior; they deepen connection and anchor students within the classroom community.

Respect preserves dignity. Students may not always respond with maturity, but they understand fairness. When misbehavior is addressed privately and calmly, dignity remains intact. Respect modeled by the teacher becomes the standard students learn to follow, shaping both behavior and relationships.

Belonging must also extend outward. Strong classroom communities include families as partners. When communication begins with positive recognition and shared purpose, trust grows beyond the classroom walls. That alignment strengthens student confidence, behavior, and commitment.

Relationships are sustained through consistent, intentional actions that quietly reaffirm care, fairness, and belonging. When relationships are maintained with consistency and heart, the classroom becomes a place where students feel secure enough to learn, challenge themselves, and become part of something larger than themselves.

Pack Leader Takeaway: Removing Labels Unlocks Growth

Developing a **Learning Mindset** shapes how students respond to challenge. When tasks feel difficult, students may freeze, withdraw, or move forward. What determines that response is not primarily ability, but belief, support, and experience. When students understand that effort matters, growth is possible, and support is present, challenge becomes navigable rather than paralyzing.

Mindset and learning styles are not static labels. Students are not rigidly fixed or growth, visual or hands-on. Learning shifts across contexts, subjects, and moments. When labels solidify, they restrict effort and shift responsibility away from the learner and onto whether instruction matches a preferred style. When labels are dismantled, students regain agency and responsibility for their learning.

One way to support that shift is by teaching students that the brain can change. Understanding neuroplasticity gives learners a concrete explanation for growth. When students see that practice strengthens neural pathways, difficulty becomes evidence of development rather than inadequacy. As a result, resignation gives way to curiosity, and frustration gives way to strategy.

Effort builds capacity. Persistence, practice, and thoughtful strategy matter more than innate talent. When students view effort as investment rather than weakness, they are more willing to try again after failure. Learning accelerates when struggle is framed as part of the process rather than proof of limitation or identity.

Care creates courage. Students take risks when they feel respected, supported, and genuinely believed in. Empathy paired with high expectations communicates partnership rather than pressure. When teachers demonstrate consistency, fairness, and reliability, students trust the learning environment enough to persist through uncertainty.

Language also shapes belief. The words teachers choose signal expectation and confidence. Inclusive language, collaborative framing, and careful questioning reinforce the idea that learning is shared work. When students hear belief in their potential, they are more likely to act on it.

Mindset grows through experience. When classrooms honor effort, teach the science of learning, and balance care with accountability, students stop defining themselves by labels and begin defining themselves by growth. That shift builds confidence, strengthens resilience, and supports a **Learning Mindset**.

Pack Leader Takeaway: Enthusiasm is Contagious

Students absorb our emotional cues long before they process our words. Tone, posture, facial expression, and movement communicate meaning instantly. Whether we intend it or not, the energy we bring spreads through the room, shaping attention, motivation, and willingness to participate. What we model emotionally becomes the climate in which students learn.

Visible enthusiasm matters because students respond to what they can see and hear. A warm tone, expressive movement, and animated delivery signal that learning is worth their attention. When enthusiasm is perceptible, boredom decreases and curiosity increases.

Belief in the content shapes belief in the learner. When teachers clearly love what they teach, students infer that the subject has value and that they are capable of engaging with it. In this way, passion frames challenge as invitation rather than obligation.

The body reinforces what the voice communicates. Movement, gesture, pacing, and facial expression signal enthusiasm and help anchor meaning.

Furthermore, when lessons incorporate story, motion, sound, and emotion, learning becomes multisensory, strengthening memory and helping ideas stick.

Enthusiasm grows from authenticity and intention. Sustained energy comes from caring deeply about the work and communicating that care consistently through small, regular expressions of joy.

Joy builds approachability. Warmth and expressive tone invite students toward learning rather than pushing them into compliance. When students feel positive emotional energy, they are more willing to take risks, ask questions, and engage fully.

The way we show up emotionally each day teaches students how to feel about learning itself. When we lead with visible joy, curiosity, and care, students experience learning as inviting, meaningful, and worthwhile.

Pack Leader Takeaway: Unleash Motivation by Meeting Needs

Motivation emerges when the learning environment meets human needs. Students work hardest when they feel connected, capable, and valued. When these conditions are present, effort sustains itself.

Belonging anchors motivation. When students feel part of a classroom community, effort gains purpose through connection. Learners persist not only for personal success, but because their work matters to others. As a result, shared responsibility deepens commitment and follow-through.

Relevance fuels engagement by answering why learning matters now. Students invest more deeply when content connects to their lives, interests, and immediate goals. These connections invite attention, reduce resistance, and turn tasks into opportunities.

Choice builds ownership. When students have voice in how they learn or demonstrate understanding, motivation shifts from compliance toward agency. Even small choices increase investment and signal trust.

Challenge sustains growth. Motivation thrives in spaces where expectations stretch students without overwhelming them. Clear goals, visible progress, and structured reflection help learners persist through difficulty and view struggle as part of learning rather than a reason to disengage.

Recognition fuels momentum. Acknowledging effort, strategy, and growth strengthens confidence and encourages continued persistence. When recognition highlights progress and process, it reinforces mastery and builds resilience.

Novelty sparks curiosity. Moments of surprise, inquiry, and creative variation refresh attention and invite exploration. In this way, curiosity keeps learning alive and helps prevent disengagement.

Purpose directs effort beyond grades and the present moment. Students work differently when learning connects to something larger than themselves. When knowledge serves future roles, real people, or shared contributions, motivation endures even when the work becomes challenging.

Teacher influence carries responsibility. We shape motivation through our words, tone, expectations, and reinforcement. Encouragement builds confidence, and careless reliance on extrinsic incentives can quietly weaken intrinsic drive. Awareness of that influence protects students' internal motivation.

Motivation is cultivated through careful intentional design. When classrooms consistently support belonging, relevance, agency, challenge, recognition, novelty, and purpose, students *want* to engage.

Pack leaders do not chase motivation. They unleash it by meeting needs.

Pack Leader Takeaway: Active Learning Directs Mental Energy

Active learning gives students' energy direction and purpose. Learners need meaningful work that invites thinking, creating, discussing, and problem solving. When energy is channeled into purposeful activity, restlessness fades and engagement rises.

Structure makes active learning possible. The routines, procedures, and relationships established earlier create the conditions that allow active learning to function smoothly. When expectations are predictable, students feel safe enough to move, talk, and think deeply about the task.

From there, pacing protects attention. Learning thrives in short, intentional intervals rather than long stretches of passive listening. Well-timed shifts between input, processing, movement, and reflection keep attention steady and sustainable. Similarly, chunking builds confidence. Breaking complex ideas into connected steps allows students to experience success early and often, helping them trust the process and persist through challenge.

Active learning also thrives on shared responsibility. Peer leadership enhances understanding when students teach, explain, and guide one another. In these moments, learning deepens for everyone involved, and the classroom shifts from teacher-centered delivery to collective ownership.

The physical environment reinforces these efforts. Seating, pathways, and access to materials silently teach expectations and shape engagement. A thoughtfully designed room reduces friction and supports collaboration before instruction even begins.

Concrete experiences further anchor learning. Hands-on work gives students an entry point into abstract ideas. When learners build, manipulate, model, or demonstrate concepts, understanding becomes more durable and transferable. Purposeful movement supports this process by refreshing focus and sustaining cognitive performance, keeping energy productive rather than disruptive.

As students engage actively, their thinking becomes visible. Writing, drawing, modeling, and discussion externalize understanding, making learning observable and improvable. In this environment, mistakes become information rather than failure.

Active instruction replaces management with momentum. When lessons engage minds and bodies, behavior follows naturally, and the classroom buzzes with focus because students are invested in the work. Students who spend class thinking deeply and contributing meaningfully leave with a sense of accomplishment and fulfillment.

Pack leaders design experiences that give energy direction, purpose, and meaning. When instruction honors how the brain learns best, students respond with focus, curiosity, and eagerness to engage.

Pack Leader Takeaway: Model Emotional Regulation

Students look to their teacher for emotional leadership. Tone, posture, and presence often communicate meaning more powerfully than words. When the teacher remains calm, cool, and collected, the classroom mirrors that stability.

Behavior is modeled through teacher self-regulation. When educators pause, breathe, and respond thoughtfully, they model the emotional control they expect from students. This regulation often shapes behavior before consequences are ever needed.

Educator authority is nonnegotiable. Power struggles weaken credibility and shift attention away from learning. When teachers refuse to engage in emotional tug-of-war, they preserve student dignity and reinforce their leadership. Confidence communicated through presence removes any invitation to challenge authority.

Student behavior must remain separate from student identity. Correcting actions while preserving relationships allows students to learn without shame. When students know that mistakes do not threaten belonging, they are more willing to reflect, repair, and improve.

For this reason, the least invasive intervention that restores expected behavior is often the most effective. Proximity, eye contact, silence, a quiet redirection, or reinforcing the expected behavior in nearby students can prevent escalation while maintaining instructional flow. These subtle actions communicate awareness and consistency without disrupting learning.

When additional support is needed, correction works best when it is scaled and intentional. Gentle redirection, reflective conversation, and restorative accountability provide a progression that reinforces expectations while protecting trust. Logical consequences teach responsibility without removing students from the learning community.

Recognition also plays a critical role. Pack leaders notice growth and reinforce improved behavior when it appears. Together, correction and acknowledgment shape a culture of accountability grounded in empathy and care.

Effective classroom management is emotional leadership. When correction is delivered with consistency, empathy, and steady authority, students learn self-control through example. The classroom remains a place of safety, structure, and growth, where behavior is guided, relationships are protected, and learning stays at the center of the pack.

Pack Leader Takeaway: New Tricks for Renewal

Classroom climates may drift over time. Small allowances and exceptions can compound, routines loosen, and expectations blur. This drift is not failure; it is a natural part of working with humans. Effective leaders notice when balance has shifted and respond with intention rather than frustration.

Resetting begins with honesty. Evaluating what is no longer working builds credibility and trust. When teachers acknowledge inconsistency and invite students into the renewal process, change becomes collaborative rather than corrective. Transparency signals leadership, not weakness.

Revisiting restores meaning. When routines and expectations are examined together, students reconnect with their purpose. Expectations regain legitimacy when students understand why they exist and how they support learning for everyone.

An effective reset should also be visible. Physical changes, such as rearranging space, adjusting seating or roles, or clearing past behavior tallies, mark a clear transition. A clean slate communicates that growth remains possible and that students are not defined by previous missteps.

Together, revisiting, resetting, and restarting reintroduce energy. A well-timed moment of joy, novelty, or shared celebration can be used to reconnect effort with positive emotion. Motivation returns when renewed expectations are paired with optimism and a steady, encouraging presence.

Renewal depends on positive emotional leadership. Teacher tone, posture, and outlook shape how students experience the reset. Optimism spreads as quickly as frustration, and the emotional current of the room follows the leader.

Pushback is a natural part of renewal. What looks like resistance is often adjustment. When teachers respond with steady consistency, empathy, and appreciation for effort, students experience the reset as supportive rather than punitive. Over time, the renewed environment becomes familiar, stable, and trusted.

Reflection and repair sustain the renewed momentum together. Pausing to assess climate, relationships, and routines prevents future drift, while acknowledging missteps and restoring relationships reinforces trust. In this way, accountability and belonging coexist. Reflection sharpens awareness, and repair models humility and resilience.

Classroom renewal protects the pack. Effective leaders balance compassion for individuals with responsibility to the group. By resetting within the classroom, teachers preserve authority, connection, and continuity of learning.

Renewal is an act of strong leadership. Choosing to revisit, reset, restart, reflect, and repair demonstrates belief in growth, for students and for ourselves. Strong classrooms are not those that never drift, but those that are guided back with clarity, compassion, and care.

Collectively, the Pack Leader Takeaways summarize something deeper than classroom management strategies. Structure, motivation, correction, and renewal all succeed or fail based on the same underlying principle: how we shape behavior matters as much as the expectations we set. Leadership that relies on fear may produce short-term compliance, but leadership grounded in trust builds lasting growth. This belief sits beneath every practice in this book, both in the classroom and at home with my canine companions. It is the foundation of positive training, a philosophy that replaces control with guidance and obedience with connection.

The Power of Positive Training

Experience shapes belief. Early in life, many of us learned that discipline meant punishment. Correction was often about control rather than growth. When I was a child, when a dog misbehaved, the expected response was to rub its nose in the accident or swat it with a rolled newspaper. Those moments taught obedience, but they also taught fear.

When I began training my own dogs as an adult, I was relieved to discover that positive behavior modification yields entirely different results. The focus shifts from what went wrong to what can go right. We reward the behavior we want, guide the behavior that needs shaping, and build trust instead of tension. The transformation is remarkable: confidence replaces fear, curiosity replaces avoidance, and genuine partnership replaces compliance.

The same truth applies to teaching. As educators, we often hear echoes of old expectations. The question, *"Where is the punishment,"* still lingers in schools. I think back to those fearful dogs from my childhood and how they would cower at the sight of a newspaper. They had learned the rules, but not security. The lesson stayed with me: fear may produce short term obedience, but it never creates lasting connections.

The students we teach today need the same trust our dogs do. They thrive when guided by encouragement, consistency, and clear limits delivered with care. Positive management does not mean permissiveness. It means reinforcing effort, acknowledging improvement, and maintaining boundaries without humiliation. It means understanding that correction can restore dignity rather than diminish it.

The difference between punishment and guidance is profound. Punishment stops behavior through fear; guidance reshapes it through understanding. Fear silences; guidance teaches. Students, like dogs, learn most effectively in environments where expectations are clear and consequences are fair. In those spaces, they take risks, recover from mistakes, and develop the confidence to keep trying.

This truth has played out in my own home for years. We have had Bella since she was eight weeks old, and we are all she has ever known. Nearly every approach in this book is one I have used with her. What amazes me most is her response to correction. If I scold her, she comes running to me. If my tone is stern, she comes running. Whatever my attitude or my words, she never retreats. She comes closer. The relationship is so strong that even when I am unhappy with her behavior, she chooses connection over distance. She *wants* to understand. She *wants* to do better. While no human would respond with quite that same eagerness, the moment still illustrates the strength of a positive approach. I have had students share, after a quiet one-on-one conversation to clear the air, how much lighter and happier they feel in class. The relationship did not break through correction; it grew because correction came with care.

When I look at my dogs now, confident, playful, and eager to please, I am reminded of the power of positivity. They do not obey out of fear but out of trust. Their behavior is rooted in relationship, not avoidance. If positive behavior management can transform canines so completely, imagine the power it holds for young, developing minds.

Positive reinforcement does more than improve behavior; it shapes the emotional climate of the classroom. It tells students that success is expected, effort is valued, and mistakes are part of learning. It replaces fear with belonging and compliance with cooperation. It creates classrooms where growth feels possible and where everyone, teacher and student alike, can breathe.

Final Reflection: Empathy Inspires Effort

Teaching is an act of leadership, and classroom management is the art that sustains it. Every chapter, every reflection, and every story in this book points to one truth: the way we lead impacts student learning. Structure, care, and consistency are not separate skills; together, they create the environment where curiosity and confidence grow.

We began this journey with wagging tails and eager hearts, exploring how planning, patience, and positive reinforcement shape behavior and build trust. Along the way, we learned that great classrooms are grounded in connection. The best teachers lead with calm, purpose, and authenticity, guiding their students toward growth through consistency and care.

Two ideas have anchored my teaching from the beginning. The first is a quote by Zig Ziglar that hung on my classroom wall: "*Do not be disappointed in the results you did not get from the work you did not do.*" Students heard it often, but it was never meant as scolding. It was an invitation to own their effort, to see the link between preparation and progress, and to understand that learning is built through practice. Together, we examined what genuine effort looked like. We talked about how success in sports, music, or gaming never comes from talent alone, but from commitment, repetition, and discipline. When students recognized that hard work was a path to mastery, they began to approach challenges differently. In essence, effort gave them agency.

The second quote guided how I led with heart. Maya Angelou once said, "*People will forget what you said, but they will never forget how you made them feel.*" That truth shaped every interaction I had with my students. Care is not softness that lowers expectations; it is the steady assurance that says, "*I believe in you, and I will walk alongside you.*" Through empathy, language, and presence, I built a classroom where students felt respected, supported, and capable. When they knew I would be fair, consistent, and honest, they met those same expectations in return. Care built courage, the courage to try, to fail, and to keep going.

Effort and empathy work together like rhythm and melody. Effort challenges students to stretch toward their potential. And, empathy assures them that they are not doing it alone. One drives growth; the other sustains it. Students flourish when both are present; when the classroom demands their best while reminding them that their worth is never tied to a grade.

As educators, we hold the power to shape those conditions. We steady storms with our calm, open minds with our enthusiasm, and change lives through our belief in what students can become. Each time we choose patience over frustration, grace over judgment, and encouragement over criticism, we strengthen both their confidence and our community.

Leadership in the classroom mirrors leadership in life. The more we listen, adapt, and reflect, the stronger our influence becomes. When we lead with empathy and consistency, students sense it. They know they are safe to grow, free to question, and supported through their mistakes. Those moments of trust will outlast every lesson plan.

Management is not a checklist to master; it is a relationship to nurture. It grows through presence, patience, and persistence. The work is demanding, but it is deeply rewarding.

In the end, effort and empathy speak the same language. Effort says, *"Keep trying."* Empathy declares, *"I've got you."* Together they whisper, *"You can achieve more than you ever thought possible."* Perhaps that is the true purpose of teaching: to help students see that their potential is only as limited as their perseverance.

Acknowledgments

Many great stories begin with a little chaos. This one started with a Doberman. Sophie, you were, without question, a pain in the butt. Your energy, your stubbornness, and your absolute refusal to do anything halfway forced me to think differently, respond intentionally, and stay consistent. Somewhere between training you and starting a new school year, the idea for this book took shape. It turns out that great ideas sometimes come wrapped in four legs and just enough mischief to keep things interesting.

To Bella, Liberty, and Bear, my steady companions while this book came to life, thank you for the daily reminders that patience and consistency are essential, and that trust is built over time. Bella, for your loyalty and quiet presence. Liberty, for showing me that it is never too late to learn something new. Bear, for teaching me that trust is earned one moment at a time. Each of you left your mark on these pages.

To my best friend, Chelle, for always being my cheerleader and my support system, and, importantly, for loaning me your dad. And to Papa, my editor, my sounding board, and my very own professor outside the classroom, thank you for reading every word with care, asking the questions that made this work stronger, and offering insight with both honesty and heart. Your guidance shaped this book in ways I could not have done alone.

To my husband, Brian, thank you for your unwavering support and your belief in me from beginning to end. You have been my rock, the one who listened when I needed to process, and the one who reminded me to keep going. You have been steady, encouraging, and always in my corner, and I am deeply grateful.

And finally, to the students I had the privilege of teaching over the past 18 years. You are the reason this book exists. You have challenged me, inspired me, and taught me lessons that stayed with me long after the moment passed. Through every interaction, every success, and every misstep, you helped shape the teacher I became. This book is a reflection of what we built together.

This journey has never been mine alone. As Robert Ingersoll reminds us, "*We rise by lifting others.*"

References

Ames, C. (1992). Classrooms: Goals, structures, and student motivation. *Journal of Educational Psychology, 84*(3), 261–271. https://doi.org/10.1037/0022-0663.84.3.261

Amstutz, L. S., & Mullet, J. H. (2015). *The little book of restorative discipline for schools: Teaching responsibility; creating caring climates.* Good Books.

Barrett, P. M., Rapee, R. M., Dadds, M. M., & Ryan, S. M. (1996). Family enhancement of cognitive style in anxious and aggressive children. *Journal of Abnormal Child Psychology, 24*(2), 187–203. https://doi.org/10.1007/bf01441484

Benner, G. J., Strycker, L. A., Ralston, N. C., Michael, E., Jolivette, K., Baylin, A., & Zeng, S. (2022). Promoting engagement of U.S. elementary students with emotional and behavioral disorders: Evidence of efficacy of the Classroom Reset program. *International Journal of Educational Research Open, 3*(2), 100122. https://doi.org/10.1016/j.ijedro.2022.100122

Bennett, R. T. (2020). *The Light in the Heart: Inspirational Thoughts for Living Your Best Life.* Author.

Blazar, D., & Kraft, M. A. (2016). Teacher and teaching effects on students' attitudes and behaviors. *Educational Evaluation and Policy Analysis, 39*(1), 146–170. https://doi.org/10.3102/0162373716670260

Burić, I., Slišković, A., & Penezić, Z. (2020). What makes teachers enthusiastic: The interplay of teachers' emotions, motivation, and personality traits. *Teaching and Teacher Education, 89,* 103008. https://doi.org/10.1016/j.tate.2019.103008

Cohen, E. G. (1994). Restructuring the classroom: Conditions for productive small groups. *Review of Educational Research, 64*(1), 1–35. https://doi.org/10.3102/00346543064001001

Cornell University Center for Teaching Innovation. (n.d.). *Collaborative learning.* Cornell University. https://teaching.cornell.edu/teaching-resources/active-collaborative-learning/collaborative-learning

Deci, E. L., & Ryan, R. M. (1985). *Intrinsic motivation and self-determination in human behavior.* Springer Science & Business Media.

Deci, E. L., & Ryan, R. M. (2000). The "What" and "Why" of Goal Pursuits: Human Needs and the Self-Determination of Behavior. *Psychological Inquiry, 11*(4), 227–268. https://doi.org/10.1207/S15327965PLI1104_01

Draganski, B., Gaser, C., Busch, V., Schuierer, G., Bogdahn, U., & May, A. (2004). Neuroplasticity: Changes in grey matter induced by training. *Nature, 427*(6972), 311–312. https://doi.org/10.1038/427311a

Dreisbach, R. H., & Robertson, W. O. (1987). Tylenol cyanide poisoning in the United States, 1982. In R. H. Dreisbach & W. O. Robertson (Eds.), *Handbook of poisoning: Prevention, diagnosis and treatment* (12th ed., pp. 215–216). Appleton & Lange.

Dweck, C. S. (1986). Motivational processes affecting learning. *American Psychologist, 41*(10), 1040–1048. https://doi.org/10.1037/0003-066X.41.10.1040

Dweck, C. S. (2006). *Mindset: The New Psychology of Success.* Random House.

Education Endowment Foundation. (2021). Collaborative learning approaches. https://educationendowmentfoundation.org.uk/education-evidence/teaching-learning-toolkit/collaborative-learning-approaches

Ericsson, A., & Pool, R. (2016). *Peak: Secrets from the new science of expertise.* Houghton Mifflin Harcourt.

Fordham Institute. (2022). How administrators can support classroom discipline. https://fordhaminstitute.org

Freeman, S., Eddy, S. L., McDonough, M., Smith, M. K., Okoroafor, N., Jordt, H., & Wenderoth, M. P. (2014). Active learning increases student performance in science, engineering, and mathematics. *Proceedings of the National Academy of Sciences, 111*(23), 8410–8415. https://doi.org/10.1073/pnas.1319030111

Frenzel, A. C., Dindar, M., Pekrun, R., Reck, C., & Marx, A. K. G. (2024). Joy is reciprocally transmitted between teachers and students: Evidence on facial mimicry in the classroom. *Learning and Instruction*, *91*, Article 101896. https://doi.org/10.1016/j.learninstruc.2024.101896

Garbe, A., Ogurlu, U., Logan, N., & Cook, P. (2020). Parents' experiences with remote education during COVID-19 school closures. *American Journal of Qualitative Research, 4*(3), 45–65. https://doi.org/10.29333/ajqr/8471

Gardner, H. (1983). *Frames of mind: The theory of multiple intelligences.* Basic Books.

GSI Teaching & Resource Center. (2023, August 29). Neuroscience and how students learn. https://gsi.berkeley.edu/gsi-guide-contents/learning-theory-research/neuroscience/

Guastella, A. J., Mitchell, P. B., & Dadds, M. R. (2008). *Oxytocin increases gaze to the eye region of human faces. Biological Psychiatry, 63*(1), 3-5. https://doi.org/10.1016/j.biopsych.2007.06.026

Hargreaves, A. (1998). The emotional practice of teaching. *Teaching and Teacher Education, 14*(8), 835–854.

Hatfield, E., Cacioppo, J. T., & Rapson, R. L. (1994). *Emotional contagion.* Cambridge University Press.

Hattie, J. (2008). *Visible Learning: A synthesis of over 800 meta-analyses relating to achievement.* Routledge.

Henderson, A. T., & Mapp, K. L. (2002). *A new wave of evidence: The impact of school, family, and community connections on student achievement.* Southwest Educational Development Laboratory.

Hertz, M. F., Kilmer, G., Cannizzaro, N., & Hargitt, C. (2021). *Chronic stress among parents during the COVID 19 pandemic.* Centers for Disease Control and Prevention. https://stacks.cdc.gov/view/cdc/108235

Hirschy, A. S., & Wilson, K. B. (2023, April 12). Using collaborative learning to elevate students' educational experiences. Faculty Focus. https://www.facultyfocus.com/articles/faculty-development/using-collaborative-learning-to-elevate-students-educational-experiences

Hulac, D., Benson, N., Nesmith, M. C., & Shervey, S. W. (2016). Using variable interval reinforcement schedules to support students in the classroom: An introduction with illustrative examples. *Journal of Educational Research and Practice, 6*(1), 90–96. https://doi.org/10.5590/JERAP.2016.06.1.06

Jennings, P. A., & Greenberg, M. T. (2009). The prosocial classroom: Teacher social and emotional competence in relation to student and classroom outcomes. *Review of Educational Research, 79*(1), 491–525. https://doi.org/10.3102/0034654308325693

Jones, V. F., & Jones, L. S. (2021). *Comprehensive Classroom Management: Creating Communities of Support and Solving Problems.* Pearson.

Kahveci, Hakkı. (2023). The Positive and Negative Effects of Teacher Attitudes and Behaviors on Student Progress. *Journal of Pedagogical Research, 7*(1). https://doi.org/10.33902/JPR.202319128

Kohn, A. (1996). *Beyond discipline: From compliance to community.* ASCD.

Kohn, A. (2018, October 26). Close the book on reading incentives. Alfie Kohn. https://www.alfiekohn.org/blogs/close-book-book/

Kounin, J. S. (1970). *Discipline and group management in classrooms.* Holt, Rinehart and Winston.

Lee, D. L., & Belfiore, P. J. (1997). Enhancing classroom performance: A review of reinforcement schedules. *Journal of Behavioral Education, 7*(2), 205–217. https://doi.org/10.1023/A:1022893125346

Li, R. (2025). Association between Parenting Stress Increase and Parental Burnout. *Advances in Educational Technology and Psychology, 9*(4). https://doi.org/10.23977/aetp.2025.090402

Li, Y., & Bates, T. C. (2019). You can't change your basic ability, but that shouldn't stop you: Fixed mindset does not translate into a fixed-effort response. *Scientific Reports, 9*(1), 1–9. https://doi.org/10.1038/s41598-019-40749-9

Lu, Y., Wei, D., & Li, Y. (2025). Teacher emotional contagion on students: Evidence from multi-method approaches. *Teaching and Teacher Education*, 155, Article 104891. https://doi.org/10.1016/j.tate.2024.104891

Maguire, E. A., Gadian, D. G., Johnsrude, I. S., Good, C. D., Ashburner, J., Frackowiak, R. S., & Frith, C. D. (2000). Navigation-related structural change in the hippocampi of taxi drivers. *Proceedings of the National Academy of Sciences, 97*(8), 4398–4403. https://doi.org/10.1073/pnas.070039597

Marye, S. (2024, January 11). Setting the Tone: 5 Approaches for a Classroom Routines Reset - Stellar Teaching Co. Stellar Teaching Co. https://www.stellarteacher.com/blog/classroom-routines-reset/

Marzano, R. J., Marzano, J. S., & Pickering, D. J. (2003). *Classroom management that works: Research-based strategies for every teacher.* Association for Supervision and Curriculum Development.

Maslow, A. H. (1943). A Theory of Human Motivation. *Psychological Review, 50,* 370–396. https://psychclassics.yorku.ca/Maslow/motivation.htm

McMillan, J. H., & Hearn, J. (2008). Student self-assessment: The key to stronger student motivation and higher achievement. *Educational Horizons, 87*(1), 40–49.

Medina, J. (2008). *Brain rules: 12 principles for surviving and thriving at work, home, and school.* Pear Press.

Nagasawa, M., Mitsui, S., En, S., Ohtani, N., Ohta, M., Sakuma, Y., Onaka, T., & Kikusui, T. (2015). *Oxytocin-gaze positive loop and the co-evolution of human–dog bonds. Science, 348*(6232), 333-336. https://doi.org/10.1126/science.1261022

Napolitan, L., & Bender, T. (2024, January 2). Tips & Tools for Resetting Behavior After a Break. Branching Minds. https://www.branchingminds.com/blog/tips-tools-for-mid-year-behavior-reset

Newton, P. M. (2015). The learning styles myth is thriving in higher education. *Frontiers in Psychology, 6,* 1908. https://doi.org/10.3389/fpsyg.2015.01908

Okray, Z., Jacob, P. F., Stern, C., Desmond, K., Otto, N., Talbot, C. B., Vargas-Gutierrez, P., & Waddell, S. (2023). Multisensory learning binds neurons into a cross-modal memory engram. *Nature, 617*(7962), 777–784. https://doi.org/10.1038/s41586-023-06013-8

Pashler, H., McDaniel, M., Rohrer, D., & Bjork, R. (2008). Learning styles: Concepts and evidence. *Psychological Science in the Public Interest, 9*(3), 105–119. https://doi.org/10.1111/j.1539-6053.2009.01038.x

Pianta, R. C., Hamre, B. K., & Allen, J. P. (2012). Teacher-Student Relationships and Engagement: Conceptualizing, measuring, and improving the capacity of classroom interactions. In S. L. Christenson et al. (Eds.), *Handbook of research on student engagement* (pp. 365–386). Springer. https://doi.org/10.1007/978-1-4614-2018-7_17

Quak, M., London, R. E., & Talsma, D. (2015). A multisensory perspective of working memory. *Frontiers in Human Neuroscience, 9.* https://doi.org/10.3389/fnhum.2015.00197

Ratey, J. J. (2008). *Spark: The revolutionary new science of exercise and the brain.* Little, Brown and Company.

Rosenshine, B. (2012). Principles of instruction: Research-based strategies that all teachers should know. American Educator, 36(1), 12–19.

Rosenthal, R., & Jacobson, L. (1968). *Pygmalion in the classroom: Teacher expectation and pupils' intellectual development.* Holt, Rinehart & Winston.

Ryan, R. M., & Deci, E. L. (2017). *Self-determination theory: Basic psychological needs in motivation, development, and wellness.* Guilford Press.

Schaffer, D. H., Poole, N. D., & Traylor, J. (2025, February 22). Cyanide toxicity. *StatPearls.* https://www.ncbi.nlm.nih.gov/books/NBK507796/

Simonsen, B., Fairbanks, S., Briesch, A., Myers, D., & Sugai, G. (2008). Evidence-based practices in classroom management: Considerations for research to practice. *Education and Treatment of Children, 31*(3), 351–380.

Siniscalchi, M., d'Ingeo, S., Fornelli, S., & Quaranta, A. (2018). Lateralized behavior and cardiac activity of dogs in response to human emotional vocalizations. *Scientific Reports, 8*, Article 77. https://doi.org/10.1038/s41598-017-18417-4

Skinner, B. F. (1953). *Science and human behavior.* Macmillan.

Sternberg, R. J. (2005). Intelligence, competence, and expertise. In A. J. Elliot & C. S. Dweck (Eds.), *Handbook of competence and motivation* (pp. 15–30). Guilford Publications.

Strauss, V. (2013, October 16). Howard Gardner: 'Multiple intelligences' are not 'learning styles.' *The Washington Post.* https://www.washingtonpost.com/news/answer-sheet/wp/2013/10/16/howard-gardner-multiple-intelligences-are-not-learning-styles

Sugai, G., & Horner, R. H. (2002). The evolution of discipline practices: School-wide positive behavior supports. *Child & Family Behavior Therapy, 24*(1–2), 23–50.

Sweller, J., Van Merriënboer, J. J. G., & Paas, F. (2019). Cognitive Architecture and Instructional Design: 20 years later. *Educational*

Psychology Review, 31(2), 261–292. https://doi.org/10.1007/s10648-019-09465-5

The Social Emotional Teacher. (2023, March 14). Blog. https://www.thesocialemotionalteacher.com/blog/

Valentín, E. M., Ruiz-Alfonso, Z., & Delgado, C. (2022). Teacher enthusiasm and students' intrinsic motivation and achievement: The mediating role of perceived autonomy support. *Frontiers in Psychology, 13*, 842521. https://doi.org/10.3389/fpsyg.2022.842521

Velez, N., Asulin-Peretz, L., & Benish-Weisman, M. (2022). Parents' perceptions of teachers' authority and parental involvement: The impact of communality. *Educational Studies, 48*(5), 635–651.

Walton, G. M., & Cohen, G. L. (2011). A brief social-belonging intervention improves academic and health outcomes of minority students. *Science, 331*(6023), 1447–1451. https://doi.org/10.1126/science.1198364

Wiśniewska-Nogaj, L. (2025). Parental burnout as a challenge for the parent-school partnership. *Multidisciplinary Journal of School Education, 14*(2 (28)), 227–244. https://doi.org/10.35765/mjse.2025.1428.12

Yan, E. M., Guo, J., & Frenzel, A. C. (2023). Students' perceptions of teacher enthusiasm: Associations with boredom and engagement. *Frontiers in Psychology, 14,* 1010557. https://doi.org/10.3389/fpsyg.2023.101055

About the Author

Dr. Shellie Harshberger is an educator, curriculum designer, and lifelong student of learning, both human and canine. With more than eighteen years in the classroom, including over a decade teaching Anatomy and Physiology, she has worked with students ranging from high school freshmen to nursing candidates preparing for high stakes licensure exams. At the heart of her work is a simple goal: to enhance the learning experience for both educators and students by making learning feel supportive, purposeful, and attainable.

Shellie holds an Ed.D. in Science Curriculum and Instruction from Indiana University, along with advanced degrees in teaching and biology. Her professional experience spans secondary education, higher education, and educational publishing, where she has served as a content creator, subject matter expert, and instructional designer for national exam preparation programs. Across these roles, she is known for blending research informed practices with practical classroom realities, always with an eye toward helping teachers feel more confident and students feel more capable.

Everything I Learned About Classroom Management I Learned in Puppy Class grew from the realization that the strategies that build calm, trust, and growth at home with dogs are strikingly similar to those that work best with students. Through stories of Bella, Liberty, Bear, and life in her own classroom, Shellie offers a compassionate approach to classroom management that prioritizes connection, consistency, and care. Her work reflects a belief that when educators feel supported and students feel seen, meaningful learning naturally follows.

When she is not teaching or writing, Shellie can usually be found designing visual learning materials, creating fine art, walking her dogs, or reflecting on the small moments that quietly shape great classrooms. She believes that strong leadership, whether of a classroom or a pack, begins with patience, understanding, and the commitment to keep showing up for those in your care.

www.ingramcontent.com/pod-product-compliance
Lightning Source LLC
La Vergne TN
LVHW010704110826
845149LV00014B/3223

* 9 7 9 8 9 9 5 9 1 7 4 0 3 *